MW00850390

# *Praise for No Mo.*

*No More Gold Stars* offers a fundamental shift in how books can be read, knowledge acquired, and our current global meta-crisis understood. It digs deep into ways mainstream learning has shaped our current world and its problems and offers a remedy—starting with ourselves and our own inner development.

—**BOWIE YIN SUM KUNG**, Co-generator, Decolonial Socioenvironmental Collective (Trueque Collective)

Now I have a framework to better understand the sources of my thinking so that I can move beyond my conditioning and embody my full potential.

—**JENDI COURTNEY**, Founder/CEO of Coursey Communications

In *No More Gold Stars*, Carol Sanford speaks directly to me—and to you, if you are seeking to shift organizations, communities, and broader cultures to be more just, alive and joyful ways of working, living, and being in our shared world. She has created a remarkable, beautiful gift here; a developmental pathway inviting all who care deeply about their role in the world to evolve nothing less than the role of our species on this planet.

—**TIM COLLINGS**, People, Culture & Sustainability Director, Hussmann Oceania; Founder, 4i Leadership.

*No More Gold Stars* holds up commonly held behaviorist and humanist perspectives to clear scrutiny and offers a way to deepen consciousness around a more ancient and affirming living systems paradigm. It provides a practical and enlivening base for developing ourselves and our lifework in service to evolving the systems we care deeply about over the long time it will take to actualize them.

—**HARKIRAN NARULLA**, Senior Strategist, The Sunrise Project; climate lawyer, economist, and policy designer, Sydney, Australia

This didn't seem like a book. It felt like an experience or an experiential workshop, led by my own thinking, personalized for me and by me.

— JANET MACALUSO, MSOD, Ed.M., CPC, Regenerative Leadership

Rarely have I experienced in book form anything so whole, completely encompassing, or holistic as my experience of my own First Nations cultural lived experiences. Until now, I had never experienced in English anything that effects a cosmological freedom of expression with such depth, wisdom, and discovery. *No More Gold Stars* offers something like my Ancestors' celestial navigation practices—an offer of ever-new horizons unfolding.

—SĒINI "SISTANATIVE" TAUMOEPEAU, Marrickville, New South Wales, Australia

*No More Gold Stars* shines a light on the prison of our own making. With uncompromising aplomb, Carol Sanford shares her personal and professional experience and offers a way to break free of the culturally ingrained insistence that we defer to experts. The intermezzos between chapters offer a step onto the path toward freeing our own minds and developing self-determination for the purpose of effecting change in the systems we're nested in, ranging from family to planet Earth. This book is the missing piece that makes Sanford's written works a whole.

—MICHELLE HALLE STERN, Principal, Up Front Regenerative Design

*No More Gold Stars* changed the way I engage with new ideas and my own learning process. I have leveled up my capacity to level up.

—TOM PALMER, FOUNDER, The Continuous Learning Company

After reading *No More Gold Stars*, I am asking a set of questions that are uniquely mine to hold in this lifetime. What Carol Sanford offers in this book has made it possible for me to see myself and my work—as a leader in the NGO and philanthropic sectors, an active member of my community, and a mother—unfolding in a much broader context. This will continue to shape my contributions long into the future.

—AVIVA LUZ ARGOTE, Senior Adviser, Faculty Learning and Development, Institute for Nonprofit Practice, Boston, Massachusetts

Carol Sanford's long-thought life's work coalesces brilliantly in a well-constructed, plain-language book. The intermezzo approach entices readers to become an active participant and beneficiary of the experiences, frameworks and premises.

—F. JOSHUA MILLMAN, AIA, Harrisburg, Pennsylvania, and Charleston, South Carolina

The existential challenges we face in our relationships with each other and other species makes the work described in *No More Gold Stars* deadly serious. At the same time, through its uplifting descriptions of joyful implementation, most notably in South Africa at the end of apartheid, *No More Gold Stars* compellingly and persistently invites self-reflection that equips the reader to undertake their own lifelong journey with intention.

—SUSAN GLADWIN, Gladwin Consulting

In *No More Gold Stars,* the latest contribution to her invaluable body of work, Carol Sanford reveals the hidden worldview that degenerated modern society's ability to solve our most complex and pressing existential problems. She also offers the essential antidote. If you believe that business has a critical role to play in creating a flourishing future, if you feel called to play a bigger role in the health of our social and planetary systems, and, especially, if you believe that you are already an enlightened leader, you must read this book.

—LARA LEE, independent director (WD-40, The Sill, Inc.), former officer (Harley-Davidson, Lowe's), value-adding governance and regenerative leadership advisor.

*No More Gold Stars* is a seminal work that debunks our deeply entrenched, and largely unexamined romance with behaviorism, replacing it with a compelling alternative—a rich epistemology centered on cultivating consciousness, discernment, and self-determination. As we face unprecedented challenges in the decades to come, our greatest work will be to unlearn the destructive patterns of thinking and being that have gotten us into this predicament and replace them with ones that offer true potential for transformation, evolution, and realizing our role as a species.

——**JOSIE PLAUT**, Associate Director, Institute for the Built Environment

I had to stop reading *No More Gold Stars*! Why? I needed to pause and reflect…a book not for absorbing ideas but for discovering ways to learn from life-long questions! A powerful instrument for shaking off mechanicalness and bringing up energy to engage in self-determining and self-managing processes as a way to lead change from a wholly different worldview!

——**SIDNEY CANO**, Founding CIO, DUIT Corporation, Mexico

If you feel frustrated by the state of our society; if you wonder why our major institutions, such as education, economy, healthcare, and democracy, are becoming increasingly ineffective and fragile every day; if you want to understand what's at the core of all of these messes, you must read this book. Sanford offers a sharp critique of how we got here but more importantly, they offer a holistic, systemic, and rigorous way out, showing how humans could reclaim their core role as conscious shapers and contributors to the evolutionary process of Life.

——**MAX SHKUD**, consultant

This book is a must read for anyone who is on a "mission to make our world a better place", by reading it you'll be able to save decades of burn out and frustration, after working hard and realizing that your effort doesn't evolve systems in the way you hoped it would. By reading this book and deeply engaging with the process of self-inquiry that it invites, you'll be able to evolve past the behaviorist paradigm which is degenerating our culture, environment, democracy, and society.

——**LAUREN TUCKER**, Lead, reNourish Studio, White Buffalo Land Trust

Rarely has a book had such a profound impact on my thinking, and on my very *ability* to *think* in a higher-order way. I can never see the world in the same way again – and thank goodness for that! Carol has done it again: humbly provided a pathway into a powerful lineage tradition that invites and demands that all of us contribute toward the world living into its full potential.

—**HEATHER PAULSEN**, Paulsen Consulting

*No More Gold Stars* is awakening so much in me. It feels very important to the world for it to be coming to the fore now. It also (no surprise) is helping me see new ways to evolve my current work.

—**LAUREN YARMUTH**, The Togetherness Practice Project Lead, Ashoka, Executive Director, Volgenau Climate Initiative

NO MORE
GOLD
STARS

Tamara Packer c/o InterOctave, Inc.
1313 196th Pl SE
Bothell, Washington 98012
www.interoctave.com

ISBN (paperback): 978-0-9893013-8-1
ISBN (ebook): 978-0-9893013-7-4

Ordering Information:
Special discounts are available on quantity purchases by corporations, associations, and others. For details, contact InterOctave at the address above.

# CAROL SANFORD

Bestselling author of *THE REGENERATIVE BUSINESS*

Ben Haggard, Developmental Editor

# NO MORE
# GOLD
# STARS

**REGENERATING CAPACITY
TO THINK FOR OURSELVES**

FOREWORDS BY
TOM PETERS, *In Search of Excellence* and TYSON YUNKAPORTA, *Sand Talk*

# ALSO BY CAROL SANFORD

*The Responsible Business: Reimagining Sustainability and Success*

*The Responsible Entrepreneur: Four Game-Changing Archetypes
for Founders, Leaders, and Impact Investors*

*The Regenerative Business: Redesign Work, Cultivate Human Potential,
Achieve Extraordinary Outcomes*

*No More Feedback: Cultivate Consciousness at Work*

*The Regenerative Life: Transform Any Organization,
Our Society, and Your Destiny*

*Indirect Work: A Regenerative Change Theory
for Businesses, Communities, Institutions and Humans*

For humans everywhere who are stepping
into our role as time binder.

# CONTENTS

# Why Two Forewords?

Each of my books attempts to highlight an insight or approach that can uplift and reconcile multiple ideas around a particular subject. My aim is to offer a view that disrupts and goes beyond the multiplicity of perspectives and controversies that seem to place good people in opposition to one another. In this spirit, whenever possible I have included two forewords from authors holding different worldviews: male and female, founder and investor, academic and boardroom. When you read these paired forewords, you witness two people connecting the content to their lives and finding different ways to make sense of a disruptive idea. For this book, I am grateful to Tom Peters and Tyson Yunkaporta for contributing two very different forewords.

Tom Peters is the best-selling coauthor of *In Search of Excellence: Lessons Learned from America's Best-Run Companies* and author of nineteen other books that have made him the leading voice in business theory for a quarter of a century. As a management consultant, he was one of the first to challenge the work of Frederick Taylor, an early twentieth-century industrial designer who conceived of workers as components within machinelike systems. Peters countered this approach with an insistence that companies should put *people first*.

Tyson Yunkaporta is an Aboriginal scholar, founder of the Indigenous Knowledge Systems Lab at Deakin University in Melbourne, and author of *Sand Talk: How Indigenous Thinking Can Save the World*, a paradigm-shifting book that brings a crucial perspective to historical and cultural issues. His work as writer, teacher, and activist focuses on applying Indigenous methods of inquiry to resolve complex issues and explore global crises, articulating a new template for living.

# A Foreword from Tom Peters

Susan Cain wrote a superb book titled *Quiet*. When I met her in person, the first words out of my mouth were, "Ms. Cain, you called me an idiot." She was startled, but then I explained what I meant. "Susan, you *told* me that I had effectively been ignoring almost half the population—the underattended, even scorned, introverts."

Well, it has happened again: "Carol Sanford, you have called me an idiot." By which I mean, as you will see, that my precious insistence on *people first* is too limited and, at times, even counterproductive.

But let's step back. I am eighty, and I have been studying organizational effectiveness since 1970—that's fifty-three years. I wrote a book called *In Search of Excellence* in 1982. It sold a lot of copies and became my ID ("the excellence guy"); subsequently, I wrote nineteen more books. In every one of these books, my clarion call has been "people first, people first, people first." I have said that I don't get it when leaders don't get it. An organization *is* its people. They are the only asset of consequence. Research says that only about 20 percent of people worldwide are engaged by their work. That is a tragedy and it is criminal, because people who *are* engaged do better work and support their peers more effectively, and they are less likely to be raw meat for those selling radical ideas.

Well, fine and dandy, but Carol Sanford's new book has turned me upside down—and that is no exaggeration. I have always wanted people to be well-trained. I wanted leaders to care about their teams. I wanted teammates to care about one another. For Carol, these might be good by-products, but they miss the key point.

Carol wants nothing less than to turn the *whole world* upside down, to change the way we teach, learn, manage people, and even govern ourselves. She argues that for one hundred years our organizing models, presumably including my own, have de facto or de jure been top-down and expert driven. In other words, we have designed our systems so that someone further up the ladder of seniority or expertise is doing our thinking for us, and that is not good for our ability to think for ourselves. While some at the top may be more enlightened than others, in the end, whether de facto or de jure, leadership is still top-down.

In all our institutions, Carol suggests (insists!) that failing to develop people's ability to think for themselves wastes 90 percent of their potential, severely limits their growth, and diminishes the quality of the work they do individually and collectively. We do not need to empower people (despite what I have always insisted); we need to create the conditions for them to learn, create, surprise us every day. We need them, based on their own intelligence and agency, to take each task and redefine it in such a way that it becomes more valuable for the company and the people it serves, so that what results is a world beater, a game changer.

Well, I came out of this incredible book 100 percent sold. It is a magnificent summa; Carol has been developing, testing, and expanding her approach for decades. Along the way, she has tested and implemented it brilliantly in many places—including in South Africa at the end of apartheid, which you will find described as a beautiful, inspiring example in these pages.

Yes, I'm eighty, but I'm excited and overwhelmed. I have never read a book quite like Carol's. My mother made me a reader by the age of five, and I have been reading madly ever since. For decades, I have consumed vast quantities of nonfiction related to my own work. I know it may sound over the moon to say that Carol Sanford's book is truly changing my life (even though there is not all that much left of it). It is dramatically changing my perspective on what I have been doing for well over the last half century. Just say "no" to *people first* as a way to up the engagement number well above today's 20 percent. Instead, say "yes" to unleashing the unimaginable potential that each of us has within us, which has been suppressed, or at least wildly constrained, by organizational models—including enlightened ones like my own.

Carol says that one hundred years of mechanical, top-down conditioning is enough. Let's make the organizational future all about the development of human capacity. I am not leading a fully staffed company anymore, but by God, I wish I were. I would love to turn my company upside down following Carol's mantras. I am not giving that many speeches anymore either, and I have vociferously asserted that my most recent book, my twentieth, was my last. But I *am* doing scores of podcasts (and posting literally thousands of tweets) and chatting up professionals here and there. Carol, I promise that never again will *people first* be the emphasis of my mutterings. I will only be talking about, well, *magic*—tapping into and encouraging the quite extraordinary but underdeveloped potential that exists inside each and every one of us. I want to see these capacities for independent and creative thought brought to bear on the task at hand, whatever that may be, so that it can be reinvented in ways that will shock me and make me smile.

I dearly hope and even pray that this book will change the world. Big words, yes, but then, this is a big book. Bravo and bless you, Carol. What a job. Whoopee!

# A Foreword from Tyson Yunkaporta

As a mongrel Indigene and hedge scholar from an antipodean backwater, I came late to the regenerative systems party, just before COVID broke. All the Buckminster Fullers and Gregory Batesons had already left, and no one was dancing anymore because everybody was either waiting for their turn to be DJ or trying to buy edibles with obscure cryptocurrencies. Carol Sanford was still up and boogying, though, and she yanked me onto the reclaimed timber dance floor with a slightly trembling but wickedly strong hand, then spun me round a few times under an upcycled disco ball.

I felt like I was trying to catch up with everyone else, to learn "proper" systems theory, since I'd written a book about my people's Indigenous knowledge systems applied to contemporary contexts and I was suddenly supposed to be an expert on all things complex and metamodern and emergent. Carol reminded me of my own contention that it was the party itself that was late—centuries late for a regenerative life embedded in land and good relation.

I noted that her many books were nudging people toward this story of the world, making meaning alongside the best people working in the worst institutions and economies. I saw a rare beast in Carol, a high-functioning contrarian with a good mind and survivable ontology. She made me laugh, and I called her Aunty because she was clearly an elder in the community I was trying to enter.

We connected very quickly and intensely, sharing a wicked sense of humor along with an understanding that respect and deference are two very different things and that hierarchies are built for small and insecure men. Our mutual aversion to coercive psychologies was, is, and always will be the foundation of our connection.

I sometimes call her Aunty Anti-Ayn because (a) we have joked in the past that she's the anti-Ayn Rand, although she laments that she never got the chance to write a steamy work of fiction; and (b) it's my trickster way of conferring a triple-A rating on her glorious mind. One day I'd like to feed all her books and talks to a robot and ask it to write her unborn novel. I can think of worse ghosts to let loose on the machine.

I don't regret that Aunty began dying shortly after our relationship began, and neither does she. As the Bard says, ALS well that ends well. The act of passing between this world and ancestral ones is never an end or an absence, and spirit keeps moving and doing its work despite the mundane timelines imposed on it by church bells and spreadsheets. Entropy is a thing, but it's not the only thing.

There are indeed more things in heaven and earth, and quite a few of them are dreamt of in my philosophy. However, just in case that's not reality and the universe is in fact a totally mechanical and secular space devoid of distributed intelligence and autopoiesis, Aunty Anti-Ayn has fired this Parthian shot, this last book, out into our world so that she can keep speaking for a while after her mouth stops working.

It annoys me when people say "parting shot," so I insist on saying *Parthian*. *Parting* denies attribution to an ancient people who deserve to be recognized. I've tried throwing a spear backward off a galloping horse, and I can tell you that's not an easy thing to do. The Parthians also would not just depart after firing missiles behind them, but usually circled back around to repeat the action over and over until the Romans gave up and went home. The Parthian shot is a metaphor I prefer to deploy when I think of Aunty's book and its metaphysical and ideological contexts. It comforts me to think of it as the sharp and pointy gift that keeps on giving.

The Parthians were also kind of bastards, though, as people must be if they're stupid enough to start up an empire of command and control. This is a poor long-term health choice for a culture; it results in a limited lifespan of five hundred years or so. So things are complicated when it comes to the world and the attractive but pathological ideologies that are killing it, and we need elder authority and elder discernment if we seek to make sense of it.

That's why Aunty is here with this analysis, this call to retire the originally well-meaning discipline of behaviorism, the psychologies and methodologies of coercion and control. We all suffer under the weight of it.

She says we're not alone.

*If you can see what I see, you can see that there's a way out.*

I don't care if that sounds exactly like what an unscrupulous guru would say because I know Carol doesn't have enough time left to brainwash me, rip me off, and make me do god-knows-what for her. There's nothing in it for her now in terms of financial or ego gain, and she's still saying the same things she's always said. That's how I'm certain she's for real. Jeez, you have to die before a fella will trust you around here…

She is full of generous praise for my work and encourages me to beware of the colonizers and grifters and bullshitters. She tells me to step up into a greater role in the global regenerative community. I don't feel like I'm ready, but she's very supportive and persistent.

Seeking to avoid intimacy, duty, and hope (which are so much harder than self-reliance, escape, and cynicism), I deflect by making jokes about Val Kilmer, an actor who is going through the same process that she is at this time. He's appearing in his final few films, including a sequel to *Top Gun*, just as Aunty is finishing her final book.

Aunty isn't familiar with his early work in *Tombstone*, but she is familiar with the historical character of Doc Holliday that he plays in that film. Doc is dying of consumption but rises from his deathbed to stand with his friend, Wyatt Earp, in a final showdown against an authoritarian mob of coercive cowboys. Aunty is happy to identify with Doc in this story, but more for the strong relationships throughout than the final blaze of glory in the climax of the narrative. Even though she hasn't seen the movie, I like to imagine her quoting some of Val's lines to me.

*I'm your huckleberry.*

or

*You're a daisy if you do!*

She's worried about me. She's concerned about bad-faith scam artists taking my people's knowledge and misrepresenting it as paleo-developmental woo, diverting millions of potential changemakers to cognitive and spiritual bypass via misplaced ancient wisdom. I assure her that's why I always throw in a bunch of silly movie references. It's hard to repackage something as "ancient and traditional" in a new-wage workshop when it's full of Al Pacino impressions and secondhand fart jokes. *Hoo haa!* She's not convinced this is the healthiest path for me to take in my engagement with regenerative economies and cultures, but she has a nice way of telling me that. Nice, but urgent.

*Sometimes our own thoughts defeat us, Tyson.*

Bless her. Her words will get me in the end—they always do. They'll get you too. She's our huckleberry.

Not Huckleberry Finn though, because that's racist as hell. See what I mean about the world being too complicated to navigate without leaning on the discernment of elders?

So please outsource your discernment to my triple-A rated Aunty Carol for a while and read this book, which I see as a pretty good state of the union address for a world that seems intent on making the book of Revelation come true.

*You're a daisy if you do.*

# Introduction

# Learning to Think for Ourselves

Here in the United States, IQ test scores have been falling for five decades. Apparently, we have been getting stupider and stupider since 1972. At the same time, ideas for addressing critical issues like climate change, racism, economic inequity, and the future of work have been slow in coming, uncreative, and ineffective. Many high-profile sources, including the White House, Pew Research, and major news outlets, are sounding the alarm that there is something profoundly wrong with how we prepare people to deal with pressing issues. They all agree that we have a problem, but the best practices they offer as solutions are based on false premises and are certain to make the situation worse.

A century ago, a group of psychologists known as *behaviorists* began promoting a radical reconceptualization of the human self and human behavior, and it has been sold to us ever since. They introduced a method for reconstructing society based on redefining what constitutes knowledge about human behavior, how this knowledge can be generated, and who is qualified to own it. In the process, they overturned a fundamental and enduring belief that had been handed down for millennia: that we can know ourselves and act as the final arbiters of what is true about us.

Since their inception, behaviorist theory and method have been successfully scaled to such an extent that they have become ubiquitous in all our lives and institutions. As a culture, we have so completely internalized behaviorist ways of thinking and working that they are now invisible to us, although they are among the primary causes of our inability to respond appropriately to the challenges we face today. We no longer look to ourselves for guidance on even the most personal aspects of our lives. Instead, we turn to experts and the internet for advice, instruction, evaluation, and confirmation.

## An Early Encounter with the Machine

My first vivid memory of being subjected to a behaviorist assessment was when I was a high school freshman in the Dallas, Texas, public school system. The department of psychology at Southern Methodist University (SMU) had initiated a research project that was responsible for administering IQ tests statewide. At the time, psychology departments around the country were ramping up to conduct universal psychological testing, having successfully sold the idea to the military and corporations in the early twentieth century. In the 1960s, testing was extended to students in lower and upper grade levels.

SMU, in collaboration with the Texas State Department of Education, chose my school because it had been integrated following the Supreme Court's *Brown v. Board of Education* ruling. They expected to find a broad array of intelligence levels in the racially and socially mixed student population, based on their assumption that race was a primary determinant of intelligence. I was selected to be part of the sample group of students who were tested. The tests were oral, and, to me as a teenager, they seemed to go on forever. The psychologists presented me with questions and graphic materials that they wanted me to respond to. I remember being completely baffled. I could not make sense of what they were asking me or comprehend why it might be important.

About a month later, my mother got a call from the school, asking her to come in for a meeting. A psychologist in the testing program told her that I had not done well on the tests. She explained to my mother that I was, in the program's parlance, "mildly retarded" or "slow" and would need special education, which they would provide. Nevertheless, the woman reassured my mother, they had a plan for me by which I could still be "productive in society."

At the time, my mother was on medication for schizophrenia, and she had a hard time understanding what she was being told. The one thing she was able to gather was that they thought there was something wrong with me. This did not compute for her. Both she and my sister were mentally ill and on medication, and as a single mother, she relied heavily on me to help her keep our lives together. In her experience, I was flexible, resilient, competent—intelligent. When the university sent her paperwork to reassign me to the special education program, she refused to sign.

Meanwhile, my homeroom teacher, who was also my debate team coach, was also presented with paperwork to place me in the program. Completely independently of my mother, with whom she never spoke about it, she also refused to sign. She knew from experience that although I might be an independent and unconventional thinker, I certainly was not slow. I blithely made my way through high school without ever realizing that I had been labeled "retarded."

I learned about the incident years later when I graduated from the University of California, Berkeley. My mother, who had flown out for the occasion, told me how glad she was that she had not bent under the considerable pressure that was applied to her by the school and the psychological team. I was dumbfounded and called my former homeroom teacher to find out if she had known anything about it. She told me about her part in the story. All I can say is that I am deeply grateful for the protection these two women afforded me. I had already been saddled with an abusive father who repeatedly told me when I was a young child how stupid I was. It was enough of a struggle to maintain my confidence in my own intelligence and agency without having these messages reinforced by a psychological testing apparatus.

This moment in my academic career represented a profound awakening for me. I knew instinctively that there was something wrong with this approach to psychology, and the conversations with my mother and former teacher confirmed this for me. I had been diagnosed as low IQ by the SMU psychologists because I did not accept their standardized assumptions about what was meaningful and important. The fact that they could not get me to think along prescribed rails laid down by their research protocol meant, obviously, that I either lacked common sense or was mentally deficient. It never occurred to them that I was an independent and self-directed thinker.

As a result of this shocking realization, I dedicated my doctoral work to finding out what was leading modern psychology down such a destructive path. In the process, I became a lifelong researcher into the dehumanizing effects of behaviorist theories and methods and a pioneer in the creation of effective alternatives.

## Lost in the Labyrinth

Modern social institutions have walked deep into the labyrinth created by industrial thinking, capitalist accretion, positivist social science, and behaviorist psychology, taking the planet and society with them. The resulting crises have left many of us desperate for a way out. I believe that there is such a way and that it can be found in the fundamental capacity for consciousness, creativity, and wisdom buried deep within human minds. Like Ariadne, whose mythical thread helped Theseus escape the labyrinth of the Cretan Minotaur, we brought this capacity into the dark with us, and we can use it to find our path back to the light.

For centuries, we have reaped material and social benefits from ways of thinking that view the cosmos as a mechanical clockwork. From this perspective, mitochondria, economies, populations, languages, and minds are all machines—decipherable, manageable, and ultimately predictable in terms of the elements and forces at work. Unfortunately, aliveness gets lost in the machine metaphor, and life suffers the consequences.

If we are to thrive and flourish as a species, and if the planet is to thrive and flourish along with us, we will need a life-affirming, life-generating philosophy that works from the infinite and evolving complexity of a vibrant world. We will need a way to dismantle and replace the life-destroying architectures of modern thought, organization, and activity. My intention in *No More Gold Stars* is to offer a seed out of which such a living systems philosophy can be evolved.

## Making Better Choices

I particularly want to speak to the wonderful, well-intentioned people who are putting so much energy into addressing the dysfunctions that they see around them. This group, for whom I have great affection and hope, is the one I find myself pitted against in battles over its unexamined assumptions about the nature and role of humans on our planet. Whether they are arguing for protecting ecosystems or dismantling social injustice, they mostly start from a set of premises that I think are not only false but dangerous. They hold to the idea that human nature is fixed and unchanging, and that therefore the purpose of cultural and social institutions is to manage it, keeping its innate destructiveness within bounds. Most well-intentioned people are unaware of the fact that this is essentially a restatement of the doctrine of original sin. It leads inevitably to the nihilistic notion that we do not belong in this world and should be expunged from what would otherwise be a paradise. In this narrative, we are slowly but steadily killing the world because, ultimately, there is nothing we can do about who we are.

I strongly reject this idea. In my view, there is no upper limit to the potential development of the human capacity for intelligence, understanding, wisdom, and compassion and of the ability to make systemically beneficial choices. The issue is that we keep failing to develop this potential because we refuse to acknowledge that it is there.

Potential is innate in everyone and everything, period. But without conscious development, human potential remains latent or even suppressed. If we want to do something to change the state of the world, we need to stop building professional disciplines and institutions that are organized around a mistaken need to control people. Instead, we urgently need to transform these disciplines and institutions into arenas dedicated to the development of human and living systems capacity. This will begin with a rededication of their focus and efforts to development of the life-affirming work for which humans are ideally suited—enabling evolution in something larger than themselves. I call this *actualizing systems*, and I believe that it is core to who we are as humans. As a species, our role on Earth is connected to our ability to recognize the innate potentials in living systems and to help them become manifested.

The job of well-intentioned people everywhere is not to limit and slow down the destructive impacts of humans. It is to redirect human energies toward amplifying their evolutionary effects. To do this, we must develop the evolution-enabling capacity in people, which involves helping them learn to see how living systems work. We very much belong to this world, and we have serious, life-affirming work to do. The alternative is a death spiral—the extinction of countless ecosystems and species, ultimately including the human species.

This failure to commit ourselves to the necessary development of human potential is unacceptable to me, and it has made me a fierce critic of the self-defeating rhetoric of the well-intentioned. I applaud their agency, their desire to stand up and do something about the world that they have inherited. But I challenge them to look at their foundational premises, which only serve to reinforce the underlying destructive processes they battle against. This has got to stop, but it can only stop when people develop enough reflective self-awareness to recognize and make better choices about the sources of their beliefs and actions. My shorthand for this is "getting people to think for themselves," and I mean it in the deepest, most radical sense. Which brings me to another personal encounter with the machine, this one with drastic effects on my life.

## Losing My PhD

Looking back over my life, it has only recently dawned on me that I have spent much of my energies tilting against one particular windmill. Again and again, I have found myself in situations where people attempted to exercise their authority over my thinking and decision making. Apparently, they could not imagine that I might be able to exercise authority over myself or have better ideas than they did about how I should educate and manage myself. That I was perceived as unruly and out-of-the-box was obvious. What has taken me longer to figure out is that I was swimming against the stream of twentieth-century culture.

When I was growing up, parents were expected to instill in their children clear beliefs about what was right and good. Parenting and educating were all about keeping kids on the straight and narrow path. This was a process of correction and conditioning because the budding ability to make their own discernments and decisions was often mistakenly perceived as misbehavior and actively discouraged. Authority was always placed outside, in the hands of teachers, doctors, managers, religious and political leaders, and other experts—anywhere but in the conscience and consciousness of the individual.

This was my background, too. I had a strict Southern Baptist upbringing in a household headed by an authoritarian father. My first marriage was to an author-itarian husband who wanted me to set aside my intellectual and career aspirations to become a quietly deferential wife and mother. I tried! We went to a counselor who told me that the problem with my marriage was my inability to submit to the will of my husband. For better or worse, my will was too strong to allow this kind of submission. My character was in some sense shaped by my resistance to having other people tell me who I was and how I should be.

The pressure to submit to external evaluation was both powerful and pervasive. While in graduate school, working on my doctorate, I encountered both subtle and overt attempts to rein in the independence of my thinking. My research was in the field of cognitive and organizational psychology, and my first significant research had to do with whether the way we educate and discipline children promotes lying. I worked with third-grade boys at a public school in Pennsylvania. Why boys? Because their teachers reported that girls at that age rarely lied, whereas boys did all the time.

We had the boys go through a set of simple, sequential arm movements and afterward asked them how they did. "It was perfect!" they nearly all reported, aware that they were being tested and needed to justify their results. Observing them from the outside, this was self-evidently false—they had trouble following the instructions and were easily distracted. "Would you like to see a film of you doing the exercise?" we asked. They watched themselves and then reiterated that they had done the assigned movements perfectly.

We did the same exercise with a second group of boys but framed the follow-up questions differently. Rather than asking them how they did, we asked them what they might do to improve the way they did the exercise. They began to try out different things: watching themselves in the mirror, watching each other, giving each other suggestions. We had removed the external arbiter of success from the situation and invited them to evaluate themselves with respect to their own idea of success. The improvement was remarkable. The teachers who participated told me that this forever changed the way they thought about teaching.

Like the rest of my doctoral work, this research project used a *hermeneutic* approach (one based on self-interpretation of events). I considered introspection to be as legitimate a source of information and insight as empirically observable phenomena. I was as interested in observing how I and others were interpreting what we were learning as I was in the data itself. I was deeply skeptical of the biases that were built into empiricism and the scientific method and of the claims to objectivity that were, from my perspective, delusional (and very similar in kind to the delusions of my third graders). I was particularly skeptical of behaviorist psychology, which claimed that the inner life of human beings was knowable only by external observation of behaviors, a repudiation of the ancient Socratic tradition that we become human by striving to know ourselves.

I was not alone in this skepticism. My doctoral work was happening at a historic moment when broad exposure to quantum theory, postmodernism, Eastern religions, and other schools of thought was causing thinkers to set aside received wisdom in order to observe and question their own assumptions and methods. My work had been accepted and approved by my doctoral committee, and some of the investigations I was making into hidden biases within research methodologies were beginning to influence my colleagues and graduate students.

Nevertheless, it all came crashing down at the last moment when my thesis advisor, Elaine Freeman Kepner, discovered that she had cancer and needed to withdraw from my committee. She was replaced by the new president of the institution, who was at the time pushing for accreditation. He summarily rejected as unscientific all research and theses that used hermeneutic, theoretical, or action research—approaches that had been respected and accepted just months before. He shared with the behaviorists (and the accrediting body) a strong desire to make psychology a scientific, rational, utterly professional discipline, and in his mind, this meant that its practice had to be uncompromisingly empirical. This conformist impulse put the final nail in the coffin of what had started as a small and innovative graduate institute with a mission to upgrade the quality of the processes used in higher education to teach people to think for themselves.

You could say that I was shut down by the built-in biases of an accreditation infrastructure based wholly on the positivist idea that truth about ourselves can be verified only in what can be observed by those outside of us. Truth, from this narrowly empirical perspective, cannot be discerned through inner reflection or subjective experience. In other words, *we cannot know ourselves!*

How ironic that the dominant approach to psychology, the study of inner states and of the soul, had by the middle of the twentieth century become completely and intentionally divorced from inner experience. To even question these epistemological assumptions about how it is possible to know ourselves and our world was to place oneself beyond the pale.

Naturally, at this point I was completely overwhelmed by the vagaries of the system, and after exploring all avenues for a reprieve, I abandoned my academic career path. I set aside my dissertation, choosing instead to apply what I had learned to organizational change processes in large companies around the world. Nevertheless, I retained my strong belief that there was something fundamentally degenerative and destructive about ways of thinking that delegitimize inner understanding, especially when they are applied to human beings and living systems. From my point of view, unconscious adherence to an expert-driven, empirical bias is the source of nearly all psychological, social, racial, political, economic, and ecological problems facing the world today.

If there is one thing that ties my personal stories together, it is that I was always unwilling to accept people's self-evident truths at face value. After all, isn't questioning one's assumptions a basic principle of intellectual honesty? From a very early age, I instinctively questioned authoritative assumptions. My father, for whom it was self-evidently obvious that Hispanic people were ignorant and inferior, called me a disobedient child and punished me brutally when I asked him why he disparaged my friends. The examiners who came to my high school and tested my IQ, for whom it was unimaginable that I would find their questions meaningless or irrelevant, called me "retarded" and wanted to banish me from my classrooms. The young scientist who took over my dissertation committee erased seven years of work because I did not accept his definition of what constituted legitimate knowledge, labeling me unscientific and a bad influence on my research colleagues.

Most of the institutions that you or I interact with have deeply internalized the belief that, to be legitimate, knowledge must be gathered empirically and verified by an expert. We have become collectively dependent on third-party, professional expertise, and in the process, our basic human capacities for self-reflection, creative intuition, and sound judgment and our tolerance for uncertainty have atrophied. We face a crisis of mental dependency, at a historic moment when the need for independent thought and innovation has never been greater.

I am not advocating know-nothingism, fabrications, conspiracy theories, or blind rejection of fact. On the contrary, I am calling for intellectual rigor, open-mindedness, and a willingness to hold our most cherished beliefs and certainties up for thoughtful scrutiny. In my lived experience, this is how we grow and evolve as human beings, and it is how we come into respectful and creative dialogue with one another. The ability to deepen and revise our understanding, in some cases over many generations, is how we build the intelligence needed to serve the ongoing evolution of living systems. But to get there, we have a lot of work to do to dismantle the pervasive—the almost universal—processes and systems that prevent us from developing our own capacity to have direct, unmediated contact with reality.

# WORKING THE INTERMEZZOS

One hazard of attempting to disrupt another person's habit of accepting authoritative assertions from experts is being mistaken for an expert oneself. Reader beware! If you find yourself accepting *No More Gold Stars*'s arguments as sound, making mental notes of key points, and sharing them with others, then you have been seduced into the very behavior I am challenging. Without intending to, you have borrowed my thinking instead of generating your own. I invite you here to stop yourself whenever you feel this urge.

To engage with *No More Gold Stars* as a self-discovery process is to become increasingly aware of how you are taking it in. Are you observing your own processes and assumptions? Are you able to trace them back to their sources? Can you see how the ideas I am presenting are interacting with your beliefs, challenging or confirming them? Are you using these observations to move upstream, questioning your belief-forming process itself?

The whole point of this book is to move us all to think for ourselves, actively and ongoingly. I sincerely hope that you will neither accept nor reject the proposals I make, but investigate them by testing them on yourself and reflecting on what shifts in you as a result. I just as sincerely hope that you will ponder on them for a long time and test them repeatedly, everywhere in your life, so that they will stay alive for you.

## INTERMEZZOS

I have inserted an *intermezzo* following each chapter to support you in your effort to remain consciously engaged with your reading process. These exercises are designed to interrupt the way you ordinarily take in information, helping you step back and become aware of what exactly is going on inside you. If you take on the intermezzos in good faith, your effort will help *regenerate* your *capacity* for self-reflection and independent critical thinking, moving you to a higher order of understanding and insight.

You might be tempted to skip the intermezzos, to speed straight through the chapters to a final destination. I encourage you to restrain yourself. Use the capacity-building questions to come into dialogue with your experience of the text. Practice intentional self-observation, the creation of conscious awareness that allows you to witness your inner state of being and your mental activity.

Each intermezzo will invite you to pause, reflect, and do a bit of journal writing in response to a set of questions. You should become increasingly discerning about the quality and validity of what you are reading. Stopping to complete each intermezzo before moving on to the next chapter, giving it your full attention, and working with the questions in writing may initiate in you an ongoing practice. You may become more self-determining regarding what you know and believe. You may teach yourself to think for yourself, consistently and with enormous positive effect, in all your future reading.

## FUNCTION, BEING, AND WILL

The first nine intermezzos are organized around three interwoven dimensions of living systems: function, being, and will. *Function* is connected to doing, and in the context of this book, it has to do with evolving our ability to understand, discern, and exercise wise judgment—the ability to truly think for ourselves.

This kind of functioning is grown by means of the development of *being* and *will*. Thoughts and actions, the *doing* aspect of our lives, derive their quality from the integrity of the being and will from which they arise. If you want to generate better, more intelligent or caring thoughts and actions, evolve the self who is producing them to develop and direct its own state of being and motivation, as needed. By working to develop function, being, and will in conjunction, we become increasingly whole and integrated human beings.

## Capacity-Regenerating Questions

Before you launch into chapter 1 and the first intermezzo, here are some preliminary questions to bring awareness to your approach to the reading.

- *Function*: As you reflect on how you are reading, where do you wish to direct your attention? How will you process the ideas presented in the chapter to get the most from them? How will you convince yourself to pause periodically to test them? Will you make notes? Do you have a journal nearby in case you want to capture an insight?

- *Being*: Which of your selves has been present as you read? For example, is it the you who is anxious to keep up with information, or the you who is looking for new tools to apply at work? Are you seeking to develop yourself through this activity? Or are you passively taking in content? On reflection, which is the self that you want to bring?

- *Will*: What larger purpose and motivation is leading you to engage with this book? What will it take to maintain consciousness of this larger purpose so that your reading has the effect that you intend?

# Chapter One

# A History of Degeneration

Have you ever wondered why, in a culture that celebrates its work ethic, most people hate their jobs? Why, in a democratic society, people dislike and distrust their government? Why social and economic inequalities seem baked in, regardless of how much education, effort, or funding we throw at trying to correct them? Why does a growing deluge of scientific information about ecological and planetary collapse generate indifference or anxiety, but no deep change in the ways we live and work? Why do wild conspiracy theories garner more trust than carefully documented research?

The source of these dilemmas can be traced back to a historic moment a hundred years ago, when modern society underwent a profound restructuring so thorough and so successful that it has become invisible to us. This was the result of a concerted, intentional, and opportunistic effort, undertaken by a small but ambitious group of psychological practitioners, to drag psychology out of its backwater status in university philosophy departments and make it a powerful field of its own. Frustrated by their inability to attract funding, recognition, or social stature, they sought to give psychology practical relevance, and they saw an opportunity to lift it out of obscurity by applying it to a range of social issues. An important part of their strategy was to bring psychological study and practice into alignment with scientific principles.

The *behaviorists*, as this group came to be known, believed that they could address the critical issues of their time, especially the tendency for societies to periodically erupt into episodes of chaos, violence, crime, and global warfare. They sought the means to create a well-ordered society, one where the more destructive behaviors of humanity could be controlled and channeled into productive purposes that would improve the material conditions of life for all people. To accomplish these ends, they proposed a new, materialist approach to psychology that was rooted in experimental research and scientific method. This would enable them to create powerful new instruments of social influence and management, turning psychology into an applied, practical discipline and emancipating it from its subordinate role as a minor branch of philosophy.

The behaviorists made a compelling case to leaders in government and industry, to university presidents, and to the press and the American public that there was a need to move fast to implement their ideas and discoveries. Social chaos was intensifying social anxieties and fueling nationalist, racist, and anti-immigrant movements, along with programs to sterilize lower-class women to prevent them from having children. The behaviorists believed that they offered a more enlightened and humane alternative to these authoritarian methods.

At the time, the behaviorist method seemed like a breakthrough, a scientifically credible answer to middle-class anxieties. But it had two serious flaws. First, behaviorism lacked a sound theoretical base. It borrowed its methods from the physical sciences and its foundational premises from experiments on animals. Because behaviorism started from an axiomatic belief that only observable behaviors and actions were appropriate subjects for psychological study, its practitioners saw no need to reflect on and critically examine the sources of their own thinking. The proof, as far as they were concerned, was provided by the results they were able to produce with research on human subjects in the field. Animals can be conditioned and, because they are animals, so can humans. Within the narrow limits of behaviorist definitions, this was logical, but it failed to even consider the question, "What happens to the humanity of humans when you treat them as animals?"

A second flaw arose from some of the personal limitations of the founders of the movement, who were perhaps more motivated by a desire for wealth, influence, and fame than by concern for scientific, moral, or ethical rigor. Rapid technological advances produced by scientific discovery had given material science an aura of invincibility, and the behaviorists were determined to catch a ride on its coattails. Just as new technologies were delivering unprecedented control over material processes, the behaviorists promised to deliver a comparable level of control over people, conditioning them to behave in predictable and predetermined ways.

## PUSHBACK

The behaviorists were ultimately the winners in a very public battle that had been roiling the community of American psychologists for the better part of a generation. Within this community, there was general agreement that psychology needed to set itself apart from philosophy, whose ongoing explorations into the nature of mind were seen as impractical and lacking utility. But there was very strong disagreement among different schools of thought about how to do this. The primary split was between those who relied on introspection as a means of studying internal experience and those who insisted on the empirical observation of outward behavior to generate data comparable to that of hard sciences like chemistry and physics.

No less a figure than William James, often referred to as "the father of American psychology," warned of the terrible potential costs of using the discipline to predict and control human behavior. From his perspective, the mind "was an adaptive organ in which consciousness is not static but a dynamic, ever-changing stream that enables the organism to survive in a capricious world."[1] He understood the ethical implications of a purely empirical and deterministic worldview in which the idea of consciousness had been abandoned. If human beings were merely the products of social circumstances, then individual self-determination and moral responsibility no longer made logical sense.[2]

Kerry W. Buckley, in his biography, *Mechanical Man: John B. Watson and the Beginnings of Behaviorism*, describes James's alarm with the direction that the new psychology was taking:

He was…troubled by the apparent willingness of the new class of professional scientists to evade the larger implications of their work and to accept the routinization of scientific inquiry. He lamented that for every psychologist with a new idea there were "a hundred who were willing to drudge patiently at some unimportant experiment…I am satisfied with a free wild nature; you seem to cherish and pursue

---

1   Kerry W. Buckley, *Mechanical Man: John B. Watson and the Beginnings of Behaviorism* (New York: The Guilford Press, 1989), Kindle edition. I am indebted to Buckley's biography, from which I have drawn background for this chapter.

2   Ibid.

an Italian garden, where all things are kept in separate compartments, and one must follow straight-ruled walks." The scientific landscape was being mapped, sectioned off, and mined by a growing number of specialists who were replacing those intellectual adventurers who had discovered the territory.[3]

Nevertheless, the empiricists were ascendant, not least because of their early insight that they could establish their utility by allying themselves with the growing movement to bring a scientific approach to education. The growing urbanization of the late nineteenth century demanded new ways to socialize children, who were no longer growing up within the tight-knit communities of rural America. Schools were promoted as the place where this would occur, supported by the professional skills of psychologists. A collective faith in material progress now included faith in social progress, to be supplied by trained professionals who could successfully fit individuals to their environments.

This behaviorist ascendancy launched a process by which we in the United States changed nearly every aspect of how we manage human affairs and, as a result, we became modern. We transformed ourselves from producers to consumers, from citizens to taxpayers, and from self-reliance to a dependence on external, verifiable authority.

## A Turbulent Time

Times of upheaval produce profound shifts in belief, culture, and ways of living. The turn of the twentieth century was just such a time, with societies spinning out of control in ways that seemed increasingly confusing, violent, and oppressive. These changes were driven in part by a vacuum of authority created as empires and theocracies fell apart. They were also driven by innovations of the ongoing Technological Revolution. The onset of industrial agriculture initiated a flood of migration from the countryside to the cities, where factory employment was booming. This newly urbanized workforce needed to be shifted from the patterns of behavior associated with small, self-employed landholders and into patterns that would enable them to operate successfully within the assembly-line systems pioneered by Henry Ford and other industrialists. One approach to this retraining in the United States

---

3    Ibid.

was the introduction of universal compulsory primary education with an emphasis on the basic skills needed by workers.

Mechanization of agriculture and the production of goods spilled over into mechanization of warfare, which during World War I yielded new levels of destruction, the need for new types of management, and a large population of traumatized veterans. At the same time, the global flu pandemic, exacerbated by increased mobility and speed of travel, placed enormous strains on civic infrastructures. These added to the general insecurity that was manifesting as crime and social unrest.

Meanwhile, the legacies of slavery continued to play out in the United States in the form of Jim Crow laws, exclusion of farm workers from new federal regulations designed to protect workers (insisted on by the southern states), White supremacy movements, mass migrations of Black people to northern cities, and widespread racism. At the same time, the eugenics movement was fostering the idea that society could be improved by encouraging procreation among its successful members and discouraging or even prohibiting it among the underclasses.

Taken together, these forces led to an almost complete breakdown of long-held assumptions about the nature of human beings and what it takes to lead and manage them. The uncertainty produced by this breakdown demanded a modern understanding of the human condition and new ways of generating stability. This created an opening for the belief that science and the technological and engineering solutions made possible by scientific discoveries were the key to creating a well-ordered and prosperous world. Given this framing, it became possible to conceive of people as interchangeable parts within the vast machinery of an industrial society and to successfully sell this idea to leaders in business and government. This is exactly what was accomplished by a generation of new professionals—engineers, urban designers, social scientists, management theorists, and psychologists.

Into this volatile mix, the introduction of behaviorist theories of psychology acted like an accelerant, creating a firestorm of change that left almost no corner of life untouched. At the time, behaviorist psychology was a fledgling discipline. John B. Watson, who is credited as its founder, was a doctoral candidate in psychology at the University of Chicago. In those days, psychology was still embedded within the field of philosophy, where it was seen as an introspective art. The University of Chicago saw an opening for direct and utilitarian application of psychology in the booming industrial economy of the era.

However, to be taken up by industry, psychology needed to discover a way to measure and predict outcomes from its methods. This led to the insight that behavior was the key because changes in behavior could be both measured and predicted, whereas concepts like consciousness and introspection could not be objectively observed and studied and therefore needed to be abandoned. This changed the game, because now psychology could establish itself as an independent scientific discipline and attract the kind of grant funding that was being poured into material sciences and engineering.

The emerging ambition to create a new science of psychology coincided with Watson's belief that behavior and reaction were the only objectively observable psychological phenomena and therefore the only appropriate subject for its study. He further believed that behaviors were determined by environment and could therefore be predicted and shaped by managing external factors. Drawing on the work of Pavlov, who was famous for conditioning dogs to salivate at the sound of a bell, Watson reasoned that humans could be similarly conditioned, offering a practical means for making behavior predictable and controllable.

On completing his doctoral program, Watson was hired by Johns Hopkins University to head its newly formed psychology department, where he was able to undertake the research that proved his hypothesis. During his time at Hopkins, in a research project that today would be considered ethically unacceptable, he successfully conditioned a young boy to be extremely afraid of small, furry animals.

Before long, Watson was dismissed from Hopkins for an ethical lapse of a different nature (an affair with his research assistant), and as it happened, he spent the rest of his career working outside of academia. One significant project was the application of his theories to the field of advertising, which led to a transformation of the industry. He designed advertising campaigns that tapped three powerful methods for human conditioning:

1. ***Reveal or invent a problem.*** Focusing people on a negative experience is a powerful way to condition them to seek an external solution to their perceived pain.

2. ***Offer a positively stimulating image as an alternative.*** To do this, he used compelling symbols (such as mothers, babies, and cowboys) that spoke directly to the emotions.

3. ***Use personal testimonies to persuade.*** He recruited famous actors and other celebrities to endorse everything from toothpaste to cigarettes.

Watson became an almost unstoppable social force, and this provided him with a platform from which to extend the application of behaviorism. He was approached by the army, which was looking for a way to improve its success rate at selecting good military leaders. He advocated an objective scientific approach based on empirical evidence that could be validated and replicated, a complete break from subjective introspection, which led to the invention of the modern IQ test. The test was paired with training and conditioning programs designed to ensure that recruits were successful in the categories of work assigned to them based on their test results.

The methods Watson introduced in his work with the military attracted the attention of industry, which, with Frederick Taylor's invention of the time-and-motion study and the assembly line, was undergoing its own technological revolution in the interface between people and machines. But it quickly became apparent that training people to play their parts within this interface would require a different kind of technology, one that Watson and the behaviorists were happy to supply. Watson created a management approach that used rewards or incentives along with punishments to elicit and reinforce desired behaviors. This was quickly adopted by businesses of every stripe. Indeed, to this day the highest paid psychologists are industrial behaviorists working within large corporations. They study behaviors that lead to success, codify standards of these desired behaviors (nowadays known as *competencies*), and design incentives and punishments that will condition employees to deliver on these standards.

Watson specifically targeted education as an ideal place to practice this new scientific method. The need for educated workers to be deployed within the new industrial economy was driving social change, especially the mandating of elementary education for all young children. From the point of view of the behaviorists, this offered an unparalleled opportunity to use scientifically valid methods to shape the thinking and behaviors of future citizens to produce an efficient, peaceful, and orderly society. Key to the progress of the nation, behaviorists believed, was the conversion of public education from a means for individual self-fulfillment to a system for channeling the energies of children toward societal goals. Rather than adapting the environment to the needs of individuals, behaviorist education would change human nature to better fit its environment by inculcating habits of right action (such as timeliness, attentiveness, obedience, and cooperation).

Working closely with John Dewey, who was laying out the principles on which the education system in the United States would be developed, Watson and his colleagues successfully advocated for the role of school psychologists. These professionals would train teachers in the methods needed to control their classrooms and elicit desired behaviors from the children in their charge. Increased professionalism and sophistication in the classroom enhanced teachers' stature, and they became trusted authorities to whom parents were persuaded to turn over pedagogical decisions (and, to some extent, child-rearing). In this way, public education on a behaviorist model created a convergence of multiple interests. Well-regulated classrooms populated by well-behaved children learning to be ideal citizens and workers were in everyone's interest, it would seem.

## SOME BACKSTORY

Watson was a driven and profoundly influential figure, and it might be helpful to know a little about what drove him. He was raised in a revivalist Baptist church, and he had a difficult and impoverished childhood. This contributed to his intense ambition to achieve financial success as well as to his deep distrust of attempts by religious and political populist leaders to exercise social control by activating irrational forces. Early on, he accepted the need for social controls but rejected what he viewed as unscientific methods.

Another strong motivator for Watson's promotion of applied behavioral psychology was his abhorrence of eugenics, a movement that had gained widespread acceptance in the United States by the early twentieth century. The eugenicists argued (with considerable political success) that characteristics such as "truth-loving, inventiveness, industry, common sense, artistic sense, love of beauty, responsibility, social instinct, and the natural sense of a square deal...are of a biological order."[4] That is, they believed that these were heritable traits passed down by superior races but lacking in inferior races. Allowing "inferior" stock to interbreed with "superior" American stock would dilute the cultural and racial homogeneity of the citizenry, contaminating the gene pool and leading to criminality, poverty, and feeblemind-

---

4    Leon J. Kamin, *The Science and Politics of I.Q.* (Mahwah, NJ: Lawrence Erlbaum Associates, 1974).

edness. (Later in the century, the same logic led the Nazis to create internment camps, whose purpose was to protect Northern European bloodlines from contamination by exterminating Jews, Roma, gays, and other classes of people that they deemed genetically inferior.)

Rather than simply engaging in genocide, eugenicists advocated a "more enlightened" approach to preventing inferior people from procreating. They proposed and sometimes succeeded in forcing sterilization and abortion on Black and Native American women, unwed mothers, and women who were developmentally delayed or living with mental illness. They also proposed to significantly limit immigration by all but Northern Europeans.

Watson passionately and persuasively argued for an alternative view: that the human mind was essentially malleable and that it was the conditions in which people were raised, not their genetic makeup, that determined their character, behavior, and capability. He claimed that any person could grow up to be a fully functioning member of society if they had the right conditioning carried out by appropriately trained practitioners. He proposed that behavioral methods, rather than the crude physical methods of eugenics, were the rational response to the dual challenges of urbanization and immigration.

Despite Watson's objection to the beliefs and methods of the eugenicists, it never occurred to him to challenge the underlying premise that control of human behavior must necessarily be external. Yet there is another possibility: the ability to exercise conscious control over one's own behavior, mentation, and creativity is an innate human capacity, one that can be developed over time. Many current social problems can be traced to the fact that, as a society, we have collectively abandoned this possibility, along with the development of psychological and educational theories based upon it.

## Mechanisms of Control

In every era, people suspect that they are living in the worst of times, when life as it has been known is breaking down. A quick scan of history, philosophy, political thought, and literature from ancient times to the present reveals the universality of this theme, which may be a natural consequence of social evolution and change. Things are always in flux—new beliefs, technologies, and institutions continuously replace old, familiar ways.

Problems arise when people respond to change and its attendant uncertainties with fear and a desire to regress, exercise control, lock life back into place. There is no question that the beginning of the twentieth century was dramatic, unstable, confusing, and even frightening. Many people were actively seeking answers to novel problems that seemed to threaten the very order of the world. But, as is so often the case when people act from fear and confusion, they are all too ready to accept solutions offered by the loudest or most charismatic voices.

Economist and Nobel laureate Herb Simon has observed that people will always gravitate toward something better than what they have, even if it is not the best or even a good solution.[5] In the first three decades of the twentieth century, what people were seeking was a way to control the accelerating and cataclysmic social changes brought on by the increasing mechanization of every aspect of life. Political movements attempted to address this sense of tumult and ongoing crisis by placing control in the hands of governments and charismatic leaders. Eugenicists attempted to manage the situation by exercising control over the gene pool and who could be born. Behaviorists offered a subtler, more flexible, and more powerful idea: conditioning initiated at an early age would make it possible for individuals in positions of authority to exercise control over the behaviors of people they were assigned to manage. No one with wealth, power, and influence enough to enter the debate considered the idea that nurturing self-control, self-management, self-accountability, and self-development might be a far better option.

In retrospect, this seems like a strange omission, given the lore of rugged individualism that undergirded the American mythos, but it is important to remember that the United States, birthplace and chief promoter of behaviorism in the world, was still a young country with a relatively undeveloped culture of philosophy and introspection. Rugged individualism itself was an expression of this immaturity. As well, the disruptions occurring in the late nineteenth and early twentieth centuries directly impacted the ability to pursue the individualist ethos. Wholesale abandonment of small farms, migration to cities, and aggregation of large numbers of indistinguishable workers within corporate enterprises created conditions that caused individualism to be perceived as a problem, not a virtue. Without a well-developed culture of introspection to draw from, this continual narrowing of opportunities for self-expression created new kinds of social pathologies. The behaviorist

---

5    Herbert A. Simon, "A Behavioral Model of Rational Choice," *The Quarterly Journal of Economics* 69, no. 1 (February 1955).

approach, which explicitly rejected introspection, was designed to address these problems by creating a model urban worker.

Behaviorism and the educational and management systems based on it were conceived to make society work in an orderly, predictable way. But, in the long run, they have failed, precisely because they take choice away from individuals. Over time, when people are not allowed to make meaningful choices or are given meaningless choices to make, their ability to choose well atrophies, along with their ability to think for themselves and to discern what is best to do in a situation. They may even lose the ability to distinguish for themselves what is true or false.

## The Unconsidered Alternative

There is a completely different set of approaches to understanding and shaping the human mind that originated thousands of years ago, starting from the premise that people can come to know themselves and manage their own development and participation in social institutions. I think of these as lineage traditions, ways of identifying and developing the potentialities of human beings that are passed down from one generation to the next by teachers and other practitioners. They directly challenge the learner to stretch, and, at their best, they always discourage dependence on authority. Such lineages can be identified in philosophical, spiritual, healing, artistic, shamanic, and even political traditions.

I have had numerous deep encounters with teachers like these over the years, and I have often heard them say, "Why are you asking us? You can find the answer inside yourself. Do you want us to do your thinking for you?" The Buddhists take this a step further, asking, "Who is the *I* asking this question?" And they instruct, "If you meet the Buddha on the road, you must kill him!" The spiritual philosopher Jiddu Krishnamurti put it in gentler terms when he warned us never to trust the teachers. He was not trying to promote paranoia and distrust. Rather, like all lineage practitioners, he was pushing us to develop our own wisdom, to see beyond the capabilities of our teachers so that we can make our own contributions to the evolution of humankind.

From my point of view, this is an admonition to choose to step into hard but rewarding work. If we make ourselves aware of what is happening inside and outside of us, learn to make sense of it, and figure out ways to alter it, then we cannot help but learn to trust ourselves. Our capacity to understand the world is innate, and with even the minimum of useful education, we can develop it ourselves. And I believe that if we are to mobilize the collective intelligence and will of our peoples to address the critical problems we face as a species, nurturing this inner work must become a primary focus of all our social institutions.

# First Intermezzo

Language is a powerful instrument for keeping us trapped in our conditioning or for freeing our ability to think for ourselves. As you move through this book, you are likely to encounter words that are unfamiliar or are used in unfamiliar ways. These are included intentionally, as a way to disrupt habitual patterns of thought and to enlarge or deepen the meaning that is available to the reader.

However, this can easily trigger an unconscious response; the reader may replace the intended meaning with another that is more comfortable. You might be doing this when you replace a word I have offered with one that seems simpler or more familiar to you or when you respond to what is written with a facile remark. "Oh yeah, I already knew that. What she's saying is just like what so-and-so says. Time to move on to the next idea." Regardless of whether an idea is familiar, the point is to take a new look at it, examining it and interrogating its sources and meaning to gain deeper understanding. Otherwise, you are on autopilot and at the mercy of your conditioning.

## Capacity-Regenerating Questions: Function

- How do you respond to unfamiliar words and ideas? What is the effect of your response on your ability to remain attentive?

- When do you notice a tendency to translate new or seemingly awkward words into ones that evoke familiar images, meanings, and associations? What is your rationale for doing this?

- On reflection, what of importance might this have caused you to miss?

# Chapter Two

# There Is an Antidote

My insights about the degenerative effects that a dependency on expertise produces in society have been hard won. After all, I was a woman seeking to lead fundamental change in large corporations at a time when women received little respect in that world. Establishing my credibility as an expert in my field was very important to me and, I assumed, to the executives who agreed to work with me. This focus on securing my own status experienced its first significant challenge when I was a consultant to Colgate South Africa during the period when apartheid was dismantled.

It was 1993, and I was working with Stelios Tsezos, Colgate's general manager for all of Africa. We were given responsibility for meeting the new constitutional mandates established by Nelson Mandela's government to promote corporate management that reflected the diverse racial makeup of the country. Many other companies had thrown up their hands in despair; they believed that it would be impossible to grow a management class from the uneducated (and sometimes illiterate) residents of the country's segregated townships, people from whom educational opportunities had been deliberately withheld by the apartheid system. We thought it was a worthwhile challenge and trusted that our approach could develop the innate talents in anyone. As it turned out, we were more right about this than we could have imagined.

The results were stunning. These Black workers outperformed any group I have ever encountered. They quickly grasped the complex systemic frameworks and processes we laid out for them, putting them immediately into practice and clamoring for more. Their intimate understanding of the political and social dynamics of their communities allowed them to innovate everything from products to modes of distribution. This immediately moved them onto a trajectory of financial growth and, within months, made Colgate South Africa one of the top-performing divisions in the company's global operations outside the United States. In the turbulence and violence engulfing their country, Colgate South Africa created an internal culture of respect and reconciliation that brought about a safe and creative oasis for all workers.

Tsezos and I had many deep conversations, trying to understand what we were witnessing. These were people without trained expertise and without status, who were not conditioned to need or even respect experts. Their capacity for self-reliance, creativity, and intellectual agility was astonishing. Eventually, Tsezos summarized his insights in a major public speech that addressed employees, suppliers, government officials, and others, in which he said,

> Intelligence doesn't come from school. In fact, in some ways intelligence can be undermined by schooling, which teaches you to rely on other people's thinking. But you've always had to think for yourselves to survive and thrive in some of the toughest conditions in the world. Because the former government gave you no support, you had to create everything for yourselves—economies, governing infrastructures, social programs, education. That's why you were able to understand and immediately respond to what we asked of you.

He closed by restating the promise he had made to Colgate employees as we began the transition process: "We will help to build a great country while building a great company."

I was fifty years old at the time, and it took me another ten years to take the full impact of this lesson to heart. In those intervening years, I continued to build a platform, publish articles and books, and deliver lectures and speeches, the expected activities of a so-called thought leader. But something was bubbling up from below the conscious threshold, demanding my attention. Why did so many people accept (or reject) the things I said *without* subjecting them to rigorous examination? I was beginning to be seen as a source of solutions and best practices, and this disturbed me deeply. I was contributing to the collective illness, whereby we never learn to think for ourselves, and I knew that something had to change. Reconsidering the workers that I had encountered in South Africa, remembering what is possible in a community that has learned to think for itself, I committed to never again do people's thinking for them.

It took me a while to unlearn the habits of expertise, to stop supplying answers, and to find ways to create the conditions necessary for fostering the capability in people to articulate the worthwhile questions that they were burning to pursue for themselves. What I had witnessed in South Africa was an extraordinary degree of personal agency on the part of the people I worked with, agency that far exceeded what I was accustomed to encountering in the United States and Europe. I realized that providing expertise is antithetical to cultivating agency, and I began seeking new ways to engage my client organizations. For example, I stopped offering organizational models and started emphasizing the use of living systems frameworks, which provide the structure for thinking but require participants to supply the content and do the thinking. I also set out to create work systems in which employees charted their own developmental paths in service to making life better for customers, turning the almost universal human desire to make meaningful contributions to others into a powerful business growth engine.

It was while I was in South Africa that I invented the concept of *promises beyond ableness*, an instrument for fostering and developing agency. As I reflected on the high degree of agency I encountered there, I realized that it was connected to the fact that everyone felt they had something at stake personally. They knew family members, friends, neighbors, and customers who were going to be directly impacted by the work we were doing inside Colgate and that this ultimately would contribute to the future success of their newly integrated country. This gave them the will and motivation to reach beyond any limitations placed on them by lack of education, social advantage, or political power. They saw opportunities to make a difference, and they grabbed them and ran.

The problem was that the resulting activity was scattered, heading in too many directions at once. To address this, we evolved promises beyond ableness as an engagement process to channel agency toward highly effective ends. The process had three core aspects. First, these promises were grounded in deep caring for specific customers, along with understanding about where they were trying to go with their lives and what was needed to help them get there. This kept the promises real and meaningful. Second, they were aligned with the overall strategies we were developing for Colgate South Africa. And third, each worker developed a clear plan for pursuing their promise, which had the additional benefit of providing the basis for recruiting resources and support from both inside and outside the company.

The guiding principle for all of this was the activation, development, and nourishment of personal agency, informed by deep caring about and commitment to the effects this agency would have on the lives of other people. Projects were sourced, designed, and led by individual workers, a profound difference from participative involvement models, in which ideas come from others and workers either choose or are delegated to carry them out. In this case, nothing was organized, researched, decided, or evaluated by an external other; it all arose directly from the people doing the work. Because workers had the sense that someone was depending on them, each promise was a powerful way to access individual agency, and at the same time, the promises kept efforts focused.

In the years following, I have seen that the sense of meaning and surge of agency that we experienced in Colgate South Africa can be generated for any company. In other words, any worker can become their own powerful engine for innovation on behalf of customers, communities, lifesheds, and the world.

## The Implications

It may be easy to miss how radical this idea is. It expresses deep faith in the inherent but undeveloped creative intelligence and drive of all people, which they can activate when their work connects them to something they believe in and care about. But a lack of faith in people's potential for intelligence and goodwill is precisely why systems of social control exist; if we cannot trust people, then we need to figure out how to control them. One of the things that keeps dysfunctional systems locked in place, whether in school boards, corporations, or certifying bodies, is that we distrust the intelligence of our fellow workers and citizens. We pigeonhole them; if they seem less than brilliant to us, we carefully constrain the arenas within which they can exercise choice to prevent them from gumming up the works.

Behaviorism is just a recent and particularly powerful manifestation of this very old practice. But behaviorism *and all other methods for establishing top-down control* undermine and sideline precisely those qualities that distinguish human beings. These include the abilities to manage ourselves with regard to some desired aim, project ourselves into an envisioned future, make strategic plans, and execute extended, complex actions. The potential to exercise these abilities is inherent in us, but unless they are developed, they tend to atrophy or remain stunted.

Behaviorism presents a double impediment to this development. It substitutes conditioning for genuine self-management, and it uses an array of rewards and punishments to elicit the desired behavior, most of which have as their subtext the implied threat of nonbelonging. The need to belong to coherent social groups is a core driver of human behavior, and when it is threatened, it commands people's attention. This means that energy that could have been dedicated to higher mental purposes is siphoned off to address the need to conform to social expectations.

The approach that we first articulated in South Africa is designed to do the opposite: to increase self-managing capacity and develop complex, higher-order thinking in every member of an organization—and ultimately every member of society. Promises beyond ableness are important because they arise from what is personally significant to an individual, but they reference a larger whole that extends beyond individual interests. They speak to our need to belong, not by threatening it but by revealing pathways to evolve our contributions to the webs of relationship within which we wish to be included. Through a promise beyond ableness, we become connected to something that matters, and this awakens will, motivation, and the sense that work and life have meaning.

Be forewarned, though. Everything I have said up to this point can easily be misunderstood, if you are reading it from a top-down perspective. I have seen groups that, having heard about my ideas, set up programs in which a committee of managers generates a list of excellent ideas for improving customer experience and invites employees to choose one that they want to promise to work on. This sort of thing makes me crazy because it so completely misses the point! If the impulse, recognition of need, ideas, commitment, planning, gathering of knowledge and resources, execution, evaluation, and iteration to make it better the second time around do not all come from the person making the promise, then we are back in the behaviorist, expert-driven paradigm. We have not created a context within which people *can and must* figure it out for themselves.

Of course, figuring things out is natural. Children figure out how to sit up, walk, speak, and feed themselves. For little persons, these represent major accomplishments, breakthroughs into hitherto unknown arenas of capability and participation that they see older people accessing. This gives them the tenacity and courage to pursue these new abilities despite what must, at times, feel like insurmountable obstacles. When they are a little older, usually around six years old, they begin to get interested in belonging to larger wholes and will seek opportunities to contribute to them (their families, for example, or their playgroups). In this way, tenacity gets translated into agency, and the desire to learn for oneself gets translated into a desire to learn for something larger.

This drive to take on things we do not understand or cannot do is inherent in each of us, but it goes to sleep unless it is connected to something compelling, something we can see is needed in a situation that we care about. Once we recognize the need and make the *promise* to do something about it, the *beyond ableness* part provides the opportunity and reason to stretch and grow. Proactively seeking to work on things we do not already know how to do may seem daunting at first, but in the long run, it is profoundly affirming, largely because it nests us into the systems of community and nature that give us life and meaning.

## Businesses as Nodes for Change

After nearly a century of behaviorism's influence on every aspect of our collective lives, it is perhaps not surprising that different factions have learned to use its methods to advance their agendas. One way of looking at the social and political polarization spreading within the United States and around the world is to see it as a battle over who gets to control what we think and believe. If, as the behaviorists theorized, our thoughts should be shaped by experts, it stands to reason that competing ideologies will eventually attempt to take control of the consensus-building machinery that shapes what we know to be real and true. Our experts and our facts versus yours.

For this reason, education, journalism, and the norms of political discourse and process, which were once thought of as arenas governed by a shared set of underlying assumptions and values, have become volatile and highly contested. They now serve as the focal points for struggles over who gets to dictate the terms around which our behaviors will be conditioned. This makes them unsuitable (or at least challenging) for the kind of deep questioning that I am advocating. There is, however, one arena that remains well-suited for this work because it has not yet been weaponized within the larger culture wars. Business, from my perspective, offers a nodal opportunity to shift the behaviorist theories and practices that are enabling these conflicts to grow.

Although business was one of the most powerful drivers for the adoption of behaviorism in the last century, it also offers an ideal place to evolve beyond behaviorist methods, to supplant and replace them with a more coherent understanding of how human beings actually work. This is because businesses, whether they are conscious of it or not, are fundamentally educational entities. No one questions the need to learn in order to fulfill one's job responsibilities, and businesses are constantly trying to upgrade the skills of their employees in order to remain innovative and competitive in fast-changing markets.

At the same time, businesses must educate those markets, along with their suppliers, distributors, and even the regulatory infrastructures within which they work. Smart businesses are always endeavoring to make themselves and their stakeholders smarter, and this process is driven by business imperatives, protecting it somewhat from the angry debates going on in editorial pages and city council meetings.

It is not particularly difficult to make the case to most business leaders that one of their greatest underutilized assets is the intelligence and creative agency of their employees. From there, it is a short step to the realization that a management philosophy based on control and conditioning is in direct opposition to unleashing the power of this intelligence and agency. What my Colgate South Africa stories demonstrate, along with all the other stories I have written over the years, is that intelligence and agency only really get developed when people are expected and enabled to think for themselves. In other words, undoing the legacy of the behaviorists and reclaiming the integrity of democratic governance is the true and necessary social contribution of companies in the twenty-first century. It is the appropriate place to invest the considerable energies of social conscience that currently drive a plethora of issue-focused movements. Businesses that are willing to make this investment will discover that it yields returns not only in terms of profit, systems, and employee retention, but also by generating beneficial ripple effects across our social and democratic institutions.

## INDIRECT WORK

One year after his election and the simultaneous ratification of South Africa's new constitution, Nelson Mandela created a special award. He wanted to recognize and call attention to Colgate's exceptionally rapid and successful fulfillment of the mandate to bring Black and other non-White workers into corporate management roles. In part, he was moved by the ripple effect these efforts were having in the adjoining townships, where Colgate employees, as part of their promises beyond ableness, were serving on governing committees and leading initiatives to address a host of social needs. The leaders coming out of Colgate were so impressive that Mandela's government began to actively recruit Colgate employees.

It is important to understand that the constitutional mandate was not about good jobs for a limited number of talented Black workers. Rather, it was about igniting a movement of Black leadership and agency to address the aspirations of a population that had been marginalized for generations. In his award speech, Mandela noted that throwing lifelong outsiders into roles of leadership, where they would have to develop themselves in order to rise to the occasion, was a powerful way to transform a nation. Colgate, he noted, was a demonstration of what becomes possible when you take this approach.

Mandela was pointing to what I now call *indirect work*. If you want to address the urgent social and environmental challenges that face a community or nation, do not work on problems, and particularly do not work on problems by bringing in experts to solve them. Instead, work on the creative intelligence, conscience, and agency of the people in this community or nation. When these are activated, the problems become solvable. When they are not activated, the same old problems (and unanticipated new ones) will always reassert themselves because the underlying conditions that produced them have not changed. Even worse, by trying to work on problems directly without growing consciousness, capability, and agency, you accelerate and exacerbate polarization, blowing it up into outbursts of resentment, lunacy, and violence.

The transitional moment in South African history turned out to provide the perfect conditions for demonstrating the validity of this idea because Black South Africans had been so little exposed to the destructive influence of behaviorist systems. They were accustomed to thinking for themselves, and they knew better than to trust outside authorities, who had always and obviously worked against their best interests. Colgate was successful at harnessing this energy because it actively cultivated people's self-determination while at the same time helping them direct and focus their efforts to produce systemically beneficial effects.

The lessons of South Africa are applicable to the many systemic problems that well-intentioned people are struggling to address in the world today—everything from racial injustice and the rollback of civil rights for women to climate change to terrorism and authoritarianism. By working on these problems directly, we can easily make them worse by trying to address symptoms rather than the root causes in people's thinking and conditioning. This is especially true if we are trying to do so from a position of superior knowledge or principles—that is, from the role of expert or moral authority. Such an approach does nothing to build people's ability to exercise their own discernment and reinforces the idea that they should depend on someone outside themselves to do it for them.

We end up with a society where people are aggregating and living their lives based on borrowed ideas, unexamined beliefs that are as often as not incoherent, contradictory, and destructive to the well-being of those who hold them. Once people have become fixed in their beliefs, they will tend to interpret any information they receive as confirmation of those beliefs. It does no good to hammer away at people with one's own better-quality facts to try to persuade them of something that they are quite certain is untrue.

Equally important, because we are ourselves subject to the same kind of attachment to belief, our efforts to persuade others only serve to further entrench conditions of polarization and animosity. When, even with the best of intentions, we try to persuade people that we are right and they are wrong about something fundamentally important, we have adopted the worldview and methods of behaviorism. We have failed to create the conditions within which people can learn to take charge of developing their own beliefs, thoughts, and behaviors.

I assume that anyone reading this book is well-intentioned and has dedicated themself to learning how to correct some aspect of the injustices and social and ecological degradation afflicting our world. Yet isn't it ironic that our best efforts just contribute to the problem? We need to stop lying to ourselves, abandon our identities as good and well-intentioned people, and let go of our attachments so that we can address what author Jared Diamond describes as "the coming collapse."[6] Our own egos get in the way of accomplishing precisely those things that we most care about. It's becoming increasingly urgent that we find new ways of thinking about how change happens. My premise about change is that building people's independent thinking capacity is, in and of itself, a social responsibility, one that will have more far-reaching and enduring consequences than any targeted effort to change material conditions.

---

6    Jared Diamond, *Collapse: How Societies Choose to Fail or Succeed* (New York: Penguin Books, 2011), Kindle edition.

# Second Intermezzo

An important aspect of thinking for ourselves is identifying the sources that have shaped our thinking over time, often without our awareness. Two hazards arise when we fail to pay attention to this. First, we can fall into the habit of trotting out old thoughts without really questioning them or where they came from. David Bohm, one of the pioneers of quantum physics, described this as *thoughting*, recycling old thoughts that we have had before or have picked up from others. He contrasted this with the much more demanding work of *thinking*, generating our own thoughts *in the moment*.

To build the inner capacity for real thinking, we learn to test the source of thoughts as they arise, asking ourselves whether they are coming from the right level of understanding. We also learn to discern whether these thoughts are appropriate and relevant to what is happening in the moment.

The second hazard arises when we simply make things up, which is a major source of the pop psychology, pop spirituality, pop ecology, and pop management theories that are so prevalent these days. It can be gratifying to the ego to think we have come up with a new idea, but such ideas are generally facile, ungrounded, and untested by lived experience.

The antidote to this is to source one's thinking in the stream of work carried on by a living lineage, such as a philosophical school with a time-tested, effective, developmental approach; non-fragmenting scientific disciplines that avoid reductionism and behaviorism; or uncolonized Indigenous teachings. I believe that genius and breakthrough insights always grow out of the fertile soil provided by the practices and understandings that any deep lineage evolves from one generation to the next.

## CAPACITY-REGENERATING QUESTIONS: FUNCTION

- What are the sources of the ideas that you are holding as you are read this book? Make a list of key beliefs or concepts that generally influence your thinking. Trace them back to their lineages or paradigms so that you can be mindful of your sourcing. Which sources would you hold if you were choosing them consciously?

- How do the two hazards—*failing to question old ideas* and *making stuff up without experience or evidence*—show up in your reading? How would you be reading differently if you were to commit yourself to discerning old assumptions and examining your sources?

- What do you need to do to honor the sources you draw ideas from? That is, insofar as your examination reveals that these are sources you want to remain faithful to, how is your thinking maintaining integrity with that which sources it?

# Chapter Three

# Start with a Theory of Knowledge

Now I want to make a truly outlandish claim: *the world's problems result from our dominant epistemologies*, our *theories of knowledge*. Epistemology is a branch of philosophy generally defined as study of the origin and nature of human knowledge, its presuppositions and bases of reliability, and its limits. In this context, I am suggesting that there is more than one way to arrive at what we know or believe and, also, that most of us do not spend enough time making ourselves *aware* of what we know and how we know it, and, by extension, what we do not or cannot know.

Do we know something because someone told it to us? Or because we read it? Or because we had an experience that we needed to make sense of and came up with an understanding about that experience on our own? Or have we extrapolated new knowledge from something we believe or something else we know? At a more meta level, do we consciously observe ourselves in these processes of forming knowledge? Are we able to observe the ways we participate in shaping our own experience of reality, and can we learn to take responsibility for this process? These are the sort of questions that philosophers address when they formulate epistemological theories of knowledge. With the right theory of knowledge, we can peel back the layers of habit, conditioning, and unexamined assumptions that are sources of most of our beliefs and therefore also the shapers of our ways of learning, designing, influencing, and teaching.

But not every theory of knowledge has the potential to be the right theory. There are three premises characteristic of the most pervasive theories of knowledge today that disqualify them for this use. First, they conceive of knowledge as discrete, transferable, and therefore acquirable. This means that knowledge and the power that comes from wielding it accumulate in the minds and lives of those with the time and resources to acquire it. Second, they tend to privilege knowledge over understanding. Whereas knowledge fragments and objectifies experience, understanding knits experience together, preserving its wholeness and giving it meaning and relevance. Third, they privilege authority, such as scientific expertise, over experience, which when illuminated by self-examination, is the source of understanding. Theories of knowledge based on these premises produce cultures that value control of access to knowledge over democratic participation, fragmentation over wholeness, and expert authority over independent thought.

## Theories of Knowledge Shape Our World

Theories of knowledge shape economies, societies, nations, and reality itself. That is to say, the way we think about what is knowable and true determines everything else that we experience. In modern secular societies, the gold standard for what is knowable and true is provided by materialist science and the scientific method. Nothing is known until it is observed and verified, usually by measurement. In theocratic societies, which can persist within largely secularized nations, what is knowable and true is determined by divine revelation, holy scripture, and the interpretation of priests or scholars. These are distinct modes of knowing, and they produce very different and often contradictory results, both in the content of what is known and in the structuring of social dynamics around knowledge.

Politically, differences in modes of knowing translate into ideological differences. From the outset, the United States has been an experiment in organizing a society around rational, scientific principles, but it has always had a secondary stream oriented toward theocracy or autocracy. In the present political moment, these competing ideologies have created profound polarization, dividing communities to such an extent that civil discourse and the creative tension it engenders are becoming increasingly difficult. Political dialogue has become hostile, even threatening, and people have naturally gathered with like-minded others in enclaves that offer harmony and relative safety.

It is easy to overlook that what makes an enclave safe is a shared theory of knowledge, a *common sense* of what we know and how we know it, what we consider reasonable, and what we can question and what we cannot. This epistemological ground allows us to build a coherent sense of reality so that when we encounter a reality that arises from a different epistemological ground, it seems incomprehensible to us. "How could they *possibly* believe that?" we ask ourselves, and then we dismiss this unintelligible other reality as either hypocritical, delusional, or dangerous.

A theory of knowledge based on materialist science has informed government policy in the United States for generations. Initiatives are expected to be evidence-based, employ best practices, and deliver measurable outcomes. Key decisions are made by qualified experts with the necessary knowledge to steer sound economic, environmental, educational, and immigration programs. Universities, think tanks, NGOs, and committees are commissioned to research the effectiveness of existing projects or to provide the basis for creating new ones. Ideally, the whole is intended to operate as one big, reasonably coordinated learning machine (allowing, of course, for the inevitable inefficiencies produced by human venality or incompetence).

Of course, all of this requires shared assumptions about reality and the purposes of government. The system starts to fall apart when these assumptions are questioned. Once a society has lost the ability to agree about what constitutes a knowable fact, it becomes virtually ungovernable. It is not enough to set up more layers of fact-checking when we no longer share a collective belief in facts. Once things have degenerated to this point, it becomes necessary to move all the way upstream to examine how we produce knowledge in the first place and to build more conscious awareness and self-determination into this process.

As a social phenomenon, business has been somewhat protected from these larger cultural and political upheavals around what is true or not. This means that a science-based theory of knowledge continues—for the most part without challenge—to dominate most aspects of our economic and work lives. The result is that we find ourselves slotted into career and professional tracks that narrow our scopes while informing our identities and attachments.

For example, we go to school to gain the up-to-date knowledge and skills required to practice a particular line of work; this is knowledge produced by researchers, theoreticians, and other experts. Organizations then hire, rank, and empower us based on our knowledge and skills. Or they decline to hire us because we lack certification regarding what yet another body of expertise has deemed the requisite knowledge and skills. In our existing economic system, knowledge is the currency that facilitates career success and mobility. As we invest increasingly more in a particular field of knowledge, we become more specialized, our economic value increases, and, over time, we become stuck on a single track.

In such a system, it makes almost no sense to embrace a lack of education. But this is exactly what Colgate South Africa did when apartheid ended. We did not attempt to encumber Black South African workers with a theory of knowledge based on external authority. As a result, they were free to trust themselves and their communities to draw from their life experiences as the raw material for business evolution. With this inner freedom, they were able with relative ease to generate understanding from the complex frameworks and thinking challenges we posed them. Their self-generated understanding produced ideas and projects that were both innovative and deeply relevant in a fast-moving and turbulent situation.

From my point of view, the business world and the education systems that feed it have their priorities upside down—they operate from a life-diminishing belief system. It is clear to me that students should not be taught knowledge to make them experts. Instead, they should be taught how thinking works and how to discover their own thinking potential. Employees should not be pigeonholed based on what they have learned in the past; they should be challenged to extend themselves (and their employers) into new arenas of understanding. Our theories of knowledge should not reinforce conformity of thought; they should unlock the potential in every human mind to see the working of life in new ways.

## Epistemology and Cosmology

Epistemology and the theories of knowledge it generates have an interesting and ambiguous relationship with cosmology, which is the study of our beliefs about what the universe is and how it works. Most people imagine epistemology flowing from cosmology: what we believe about the nature of the universe and how it works determines how we know what is true and false. But there came a moment in my own life when I had a profound insight that flipped this order forever in my thinking. I realized that our cosmologies are something we make for ourselves.

I now think of humans as cosmology-generating beings. Most of the time we are unconscious of the formation of our core beliefs about reality and the paradigms that systematize them. When we operate with an information-based and expert-driven theory of knowledge, regardless of whether the information is generated by scientific research or divine revelation, our cosmology is handed to us. We learn it from our parents, teachers, mentors, media, pastors, and so on. If we are unconscious of the theory of knowledge at work, then the cosmology is a given.

But the alternative exists to assume that cosmology is something that we have adopted and can therefore shape and evolve through conscious discernment, based on our own questioning and lived experiences. Then we are operating in a living systems theory of knowledge. Our cosmology is not a given; it is something we need to work at, actively, from a place of open inquiry, throughout our lives.

I came to this insight over several formative years when I was a young adult. My first awareness of cosmology as a rigid and unbending frame came during a Bible class at Hardin-Simmons University, a Southern Baptist institution in Abilene, Texas, where I was an undergraduate. During a discussion of the Old Testament, I asked my professor why a woman needed to give way to her husband in all things. He answered me sharply that this question was not allowed. "Why not?" I wanted to know. "Because this is the word of God and you are not to question it," he answered. When I continued to argue, he suspended me from class, gave me an F, and prohibited me from retaking the class in the future—actions that eventually led me to drop out of the university.

I was stunned to encounter in such a raw form the way a belief system narrows the scope of mental activity. Nowadays, we recognize this as fundamentalism, but at the time, I was mostly struck by how I was being asked to force my active mind into a small box.

Having transferred to the University of California, Berkeley, I joined a vibrant post-lecture discussion group made up of a diverse mix of U.S. American and international students. We gathered at the Ratskeller on Telegraph Avenue, a popular watering hole celebrated for the way it encouraged intellectual and cultural currents to intersect. The group was led by Thomas Kuhn, a visiting scholar and historian of scientific philosophy, who is now widely known for introducing the concept of the paradigm shift. One night he asked us what religion we had grown up in. As we went around the circle, we found that we represented widely divergent schools of thought arising within Judaism, Christianity, Islam, Hinduism, Buddhism, and atheism.

Kuhn was interested in how different paradigms shaped our thinking and world-views. But I was struck by something else. I was beginning to see that the paradigms people were holding had a source. In almost every case, we were being shaped by our families, teachers, and cultures. My Baptist minister professor had been seeking to shape my thinking, and I had reacted very strongly to what I experienced as his coercion. That evening in the Ratskeller, I began to see that the shaping was going on all the time, everywhere I looked.

From here, it was a short step to the realization that if I and what I believed were being shaped, then I could be the one doing the shaping. I think it was another encounter with someone's overt effort to shape my paradigm that finally got this to click for me. In my late twenties, with two children at home, I decided that I wanted to create my own small business, called COPYCAT, that would translate designer runway fashions and fabrics into patterns that women could sew for themselves.

My husband at the time was strongly, even aggressively, opposed to me working, and once again I found myself up against an outside other who was trying to shape the way I thought. But this time, I was able to consciously observe the process and the effect it was having on me. I could watch the opinion I was being encouraged to adopt and the opinion I held and then ask myself how they were different and what the source of the difference was. This experience allowed me to build an increasingly coherent worldview, one that I had chosen and constructed for myself. It also enabled me to see clearly that the formation of our cosmologies could be something we took responsibility for, and that the key to this was a theory of knowledge that carefully examined the sourcing of what we believed we knew. Cosmology is a process, not a thing, and we have the option to engage with it consciously.

When I evolved beyond my identification with the specifics of my religious upbringing, I became a seeker, looking for another source of certainty and identity that could fill the void. But my insights into cosmology formation encouraged me to let go of my drive to have an answer I could cling to. It gave me the intellectual and emotional basis from which to embrace uncertainty as a way to live dynamically in a living world and to think freely without becoming attached to my own thoughts.

## The Role of Humans on Earth

It is probably apparent that I consider epistemology to be central to the urgent problem of helping human beings come into harmony with a living world. This is a belief formed from a lifetime of trying to swim upstream in order to understand the sources of my own thinking and life experience. But I have not yet been explicit about why I think it is so important.

Yes, we need people to become more independent-minded and better able to think for themselves. An authoritarian theory of knowledge can source profoundly evil or destructive phenomena—the Spanish Inquisition, slavery, and colonialism are some historical examples. Behaviorist practices, which also arise from an authoritarian theory of knowledge, are a less extreme example, although they fall within this continuum. At the same time, there have always been theories of knowledge that insisted upon self-knowledge and wisdom sourced by inner development—the irony of Socrates, the rigors of shamanic practice, and the teaching methods of so many Indigenous peoples. Although these approaches have mostly been eclipsed by authoritarian theories, they still provide a basis for relearning how to come into alignment with living systems.

I believe that we keep creating systemic issues and breakdowns because we fail to understand the role of humans as a species on our planet. A majority of societies in the world, including the wealthiest and most powerful, have forgotten how to shape thinking and action to the imperatives of life itself. Life demands of us theories of knowing that engage with how to understand the workings of change, dynamism, nested relatedness, and the distinctiveness (the non-genericness) of every individual living being. Our modern cosmologies and theories of knowledge, especially the rationalist and materialist version embedded in the scientific method, are poorly equipped to address these questions. The time has come for a new mindfulness about the formation, practice, and effects of our theories of knowledge.

There are multiple useful ways to think about the planetary role of humans. For now, I want to focus on *time binding*, a concept introduced by theoretician Alfred Korzybski as part of his larger articulation of general semantics. Korzybski believed that the failure of modern people to understand the role of humans needed to be addressed because it was leading to social dysfunction and mental illness. He made a general distinction between the roles of plants, animals, and humans. The role of plants is to bind *energies*—solar and hydrological energy, nutrient flows, etcetera—

making them available to ecological systems in specific places. The role of animals is to bind *space* by moving physical material around and knitting it together at higher orders of coherence as places.

Humans bind *time* through their ability to remember and analyze the past and to project consequences into the future. They can pass ideas and insights along from generation to generation through a host of cultural means—such as storytelling, writing, dance, graphic symbols, and mathematical formulations. This gives humans a unique role within evolutionary processes as carriers of an accumulated wealth of complex understanding that is independent of DNA, where biological information and advances are usually collected and stored.

For Korzybski, this time-binding capability enabled humans to learn from the past in order to exercise good judgment about the present and the future. His premise was that, insofar as we remember to engage in time binding, each subsequent generation will become wiser. On the other hand, if we fail to do this fundamental work, we will find ourselves less and less able to understand, let alone work creatively with, an increasingly complex world.

## Deep Time Binding

When I first encountered this concept of Korzybski's, I found it both illuminating and incomplete. He placed emphasis on the collective, multigenerational aspects of time binding but failed to explore its implications for individuals. In my experience, development of time-binding capabilities at an individual level is key to regenerating the practice of time binding at a collective level. But this development requires an appropriate theory of knowledge.

We can study the culturally determined great thinkers of the past or present, but to do so without critical discernment, reflective self-awareness, and conscious intent is to engage in a practice wherein knowledge is established by an argument from authority. The resulting time binding is shallow: "I know this because [Aristotle, Saint Paul, Benjamin Franklin, Albert Einstein] said it."

On the other hand, we can strive to bring the ideas of these great thinkers to life in ourselves, probing them for their underlying assumptions, testing them against our experience, using them to challenge our beliefs and habits of thought. When we do this, we bring something from ourselves into the process, contributing our own experience and understanding to questions that humans have been wrestling with for generations. This gives a taste of what I mean by deep time binding, the kind that keeps inquiry alive and meaningful across generations.

Each of us has the potential to pursue what I call a *long-thought process*, in which we wrestle with a long-standing, fundamental question that will engage us for our lifetime and will engage the human species for generations to come. If we are faithful to it, our understanding of this question will deepen and complexify as we mature from youthful energy and enthusiasm to adult contribution to the ripening wisdom of old age. In this way, the species task of time binding can occur even within our own lifetimes, in the evolution and refinement of our distinctive work.

If you look back over your life, you may recognize that there is some deep question that you come back to over and over again, a question that seems to require ever more consideration and insight on your part. In my case, the question is, "What role do humans play in the evolution of living systems, and what are the capabilities and infrastructures needed to carry it out?"

Of course, for many of us, the underlying question is unconscious or asleep. If you wanted to articulate your own, what would you be looking for? There are three criteria that I think set the bar high enough to be worthy of this kind of lifelong dedication. First, your question should not come from you or me; it should arise from a universal source, one recognizable as valid or relevant and useful to all. The universal source of my question, for example, was the constant yearning that humans experience for a sense of meaning and purpose in life. I am awakened by this yearning to the possibility that life has evolved human consciousness for a reason.

Second, it does not ask what to do; it encourages understanding—a breakthrough understanding that includes insight into how something works and will open a field of higher-level opportunities with which many people can engage. Third, your effort to answer this question must contribute to the evolution of the human species. It needs to unleash paradigm-shattering work that allows us to leapfrog over the current limits to our thinking.

Embedded in the way I have described, the purpose and criteria for articulating a long-thought question is a distinct epistemological perspective. The dominant contemporary theory of thinking in the United States assumes that it is possible to build knowledge over time, along with the answers and certainty that it provides. From this point of view, everything about the world can be known, and our job is to acquire enough of this information to establish a working relationship with things as they are. Experts, we might say, are the stewards of this accumulated knowledge. Given that this is the agreed-upon collective enterprise of our culture, it is not surprising that nearly everyone wants to play. For me, even the concept of lifelong learning falls into this trap—it assumes that we can take our acquired knowledge and experience, our pile of facts, and continue to build on it as we move through our lives.

I start from a different premise. To grow and evolve, each of us needs to learn how to set aside, overcome, even blow up what we believe we know now and develop ease with living life as exploration and continual questioning. I translate this into a personal principle that I endeavor mightily to live up to: never do anything the same way twice; never think about anything the same way twice.

# Third Intermezzo

To make our physical and mental activities less machinelike, we must hold the intention to deepen our understanding and wisdom regarding how to conduct them and what they might create. We also need to find ways to consciously witness their outcomes. Much of what we think and do arises from our conditioning—we are often on autopilot. Thus, very little of what we spend our lives on contributes to development of our self-direction and independence of thought. The challenge is to make a practice of seeking to upgrade our activities so that they become instruments of our ongoing development.

## Capacity-Regenerating Questions: Function

- Looking back on the chapters that you have read, bring to mind someone who would disagree with something that I have written. Thinking from their perspective, write a short statement of why they would disagree with me.

- Then, thinking from my perspective, write a short statement of how I would probably respond.

- Develop and then articulate your own perspective on this subject.

- Finally, reflect on the contribution this exercise has made to your understanding of how you have been reading and how you have been thinking as you read.

# Chapter Four

# A Living Theory of Knowledge

In its ambition to create a purely materialist description of human psychology, behaviorism adopted what I consider a flawed, unsubstantiated, and deeply destructive set of five beliefs about human beings.

*First*, humans are not naturally introspective, and most people cannot develop habits of introspection. Thus, we cannot accurately observe or describe what is going on inside of us. *Second*, human consciousness and the ability to self-manage do not exist, and this means that human agency, which depends on having a conscious purpose, is an illusion. *Third*, all human behavior is the result of intentional or unintentional conditioning, and a functioning society needs to bring this conditioning under its orderly and scientific control. *Fourth*, psychologists with the appropriate training and expertise should be responsible for managing conditioning processes across society. And *fifth*, empirical assessment requires specialized instruments to accurately measure and quantify human intelligence and behavior; they must be designed and administered by experts who can deploy them in correct and unbiased ways.

These inhumane and dystopian beliefs have provided the foundation for nearly all the social infrastructures that we have built during the last hundred years. An organized and certified class of experts has assembled bodies of specialized knowledge and co-opted decision-making authority in almost every cultural realm. Behaviorism influences education and corporate employment, advertising and scientific research, traffic engineering and monetary policy, and parenting and personal health. It has had a profoundly corrosive effect on democracy, which requires the participation of citizens who are free, educated, and independent thinkers.

To be fair, the behaviorists were not malicious, and they operated from arguably good intentions. They were trying to introduce a rational basis for dealing with problems of industrial society that appeared to be undermining safety and social cohesion. But their ideas and approaches produced myriad side effects, which today appear worse than the problems they were intended to cure.

Behaviorists applied principles derived from research on animals directly to the conditioning of people, neglecting to consider the unique mental capacities associated with the frontal lobe of the human brain. Their methods worked because, after all, we are also animals and can be conditioned. But, in the process, higher mental activity was consistently discounted and underdeveloped. Thus, we have lost the ability to think for ourselves because the systems and processes that make up much of modern life have been, perhaps unintentionally, designed in ways that undermine our mental processes. These systems and processes condition us to accept without question the statements that are put in front of us by influencers and leaders, diminishing our confidence in our thinking capabilities and discouraging challenges to expert opinion.

This state of affairs did not occur overnight. It was built up slowly by means of a dedicated, decades-long campaign that included everything from advertising to educational reform to adoption of standardized metrics and best practices across most fields of endeavor. To regain the ability to think for ourselves will require an equally dedicated effort to dismantle our collective sense of dependency and inadequacy, and then to develop the systemic thinking capacity needed to exercise meaningful agency in our lives and the world.

## REGAINING OUR AGENCY

Many of the problems I see in the present moment stem from the failure of human beings to exercise their agency as conscious actors within an evolving world. Our capacity for consciousness has been undermined by machinelike educational and social systems, whose intended purpose is to help us to adapt to an industrialized world. Currently, almost all of us operate from unexamined beliefs about the world dictated by the news media, peer groups, academic institutions, and long-standing cultural agreements.

One of the fortuitous by-products of the emergence of "alternative facts" into our political discourse is that it shines a spotlight on how ubiquitous this problem has become. My news sources may have good reputations and well-trained fact-checkers, but this does not make it okay for me to accept their reporting and conclusions without examining them—no more than it would be okay for me to swallow the latest online conspiracy theories whole. The problem in both cases is that we have little experience with this kind of rigorous self-examination and no coherent method for doing it.

It is imperative that we find a new basis from which to organize our societies and our relationships to the dynamic complexities of a living planet. This means that we will need to embrace a completely different approach, one that enables and requires us to become increasingly self-determining regarding our beliefs, thoughts, and actions. By *self-determining*, I mean having the ability to exercise free and active will in the choice of what we think, how we think, and therefore how we behave and the effects we produce in the world.

I am not talking about egotism, although the idea of self-determination is sometimes confused with being self-centered or self-absorbed. On the contrary, conscious self-determination requires seeing oneself as an open system, nested and embedded in other living systems. We develop the ability to be an evolutionary instrument in an evolving world when we dedicate our will to serve the potential of the larger wholes that seek to express themselves through us. This is what it means to be a living expression of life on the planet. It is an ancient spiritual insight that a person becomes truly themself, and therefore self-determining, when they surrender the idea that they are a separate entity at the center of everything around them.

## A Framework for Describing Theories of Knowledge

Working with dynamic or living systems frameworks is a core aspect of the self-determination theory of knowledge. Most of us are accustomed to using some sort of structure to help us organize and bring order to our thinking. These structures usually take the form of mental models, such as Venn diagrams, critical path charts, SWOT analyses, Gantt charts, Maslow's hierarchy of needs, or even something as simple as a pros-and-cons list for a proposed course of action. Although they are useful, mental models are derived from a theory based on acquisition, transfer, and management of knowledge and are thus designed as tools for collecting and sorting information, rather than developing understanding.

By contrast, I work with *frameworks* whose purpose is to activate ongoing inquiry into the underlying and innate patterns of change that are the hallmark of living systems. Frameworks constellate multiple perspectives and, when used appropriately, can bring dimensionality and increasing understanding to a subject. Their appropriate use depends on our commitment to setting aside old thoughts or insights and seeking new understanding each time we apply them. Otherwise, we can easily collapse them into mental models and mnemonic devices.

A *tetrad* (Figure 1) is a powerful framework for understanding and describing the interacting energies that are the sources for any activity. In this case, I will use a tetrad to reveal some of the underlying differences between two theories of knowledge. A tetrad has four terms.

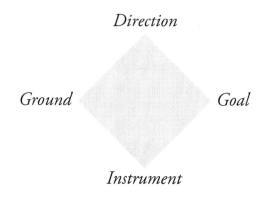

*Direction*

*Ground*               *Goal*

*Instrument*

**Figure 1: Tetrad Framework.**

*Ground* refers to the initiation point, a starting place with the highest conceivable potential given one's current best understanding of the situation and how the world works. For example, if I were planning a reunion for my extended family, I might start with the premise that gathering us together for a few days has the potential to regenerate our connections with one another. *Goal* refers to the transformation of a system's state that enables it to pursue new orders or natures of work and effect. My goal for the reunion might be to extend the meaning of who we are as a family and the contributions we could make to the world based on our collective identity and history.

*Direction* refers to the way one brings spirit into efforts to provide guidance and a sense of aspiration, lifting oneself beyond the constraints of existence. In any reunion, my sincere desire would be that the shared experience of our bonds of relationship and a sense of common purpose would strengthen the spirit of my family members. *Instrument* refers to the specific methods and means by which one pursues what one has set out to do, consistent with the other three terms of the framework. As an instrument for discovering new potential with my family, I might take the opportunity to cocreate new rituals of celebration or cooking shared meals or storytelling; together, we might also seek ways to bring new life to long-established ways of being together.

With this brief description as background, we can use the tetrad to describe the two contrasting epistemologies—external-authority and self-determination—that have been our focus in previous chapters. The point of this exploration is to make each theory more dynamic and dimensional in our minds so that we can see it at work and more clearly understand its societal effects and consequences.

## EXTERNAL-AUTHORITY THEORY OF KNOWLEDGE

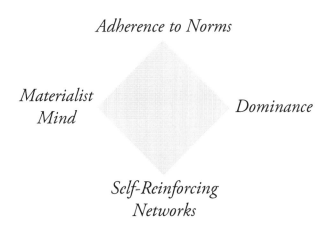

**Figure 2: External-Authority Theory of Knowledge Tetrad.**

*Ground:* The external-authority theory of knowledge is grounded in the *materialist mind*, which believes that the world can be broken apart, measured, known, and rationally managed. From this perspective, the knowledge produced by materialist science becomes the domain of credentialed experts who are the only reliable sources for what is true. If we are committed to mastering a subject, anything that has not been tested and proven by sound, authoritative methods should be excluded from our consideration.

*Goal:* Our goal becomes getting to the top in order to achieve *dominance* in our professions, organizations, markets, and governing bodies. Our mantras are *be the best at what you do* and *own your space*. We follow and learn from the experts because we hope at some point to supersede them. Very few of us will not feel a twinge of envy when we lose a competition to make it onto a ten-best list, especially if we believe we belong on it. In this world, our lives derive their meaning from self-referential, materialistic successes, which sets us up to be sensitive to external behavioral cues. The rewards we seek depend on approval and advancement by those who have power over us.

*Direction:* In times and places governed by the external-authority theory of knowledge, people strive for *adherence to norms*, seeking validation from sources outside themselves. Thus, they allow their families, communities, media environments, and cultural traditions to make their choices for them, ensuring that they will appear normal, safely indistinguishable from their peers. Social cues enable them to quickly assess the validity of new information. *Does it fit within my group's beliefs and covenants concerning what qualifies as legitimate content?* For someone who wishes to flourish and excel within a particular arena—as a pop star, for example, or a scientific thinker—it is critical to remain within the range of acceptable modes of expression or learning. For the pop star, "Is my performance bold enough to pass muster with my fans?" Or, for the scientist, "Have I been careful to limit my research to only those sources and learning processes that are deemed authoritative by my peers?"

*Instrument:* As its primary instrument, an external-authority theory uses *self-reinforcing networks* of knowledge and information exchange that are deemed legitimate by the social groups they are intended to serve. These networks are designed to collect, preserve, and augment not just ideas but also sources and methods that mirror and reinforce the underlying cosmology of their members. As has often been observed, the rise of social media accelerates the development of such networks while isolating them and setting them at odds with one another.

The interactions among these four terms create a social construct that is self-reinforcing, not only as a system of beliefs and ideas, but as a mechanism for regulating how one is allowed to engage with and question this system. Those operating within the construct become less and less able to shift their perspective in order to take in and test new ideas or to extend the construct's boundaries of permissible discourse. The construct offers no basis for critical examination of its underlying axioms and methods, because mental energy is dedicated to discerning what falls within and without its boundaries.

## Self-Determination Theory of Knowledge

That we need a theory of knowledge is self-evident—without one, we become completely unable to bring order to our mental activities. But as is becoming clear, the dominant external-authority theory we are using is toxic.

By contrast, self-determination requires us to continually question the sources of our ideas, beliefs, and methods so that we can be truly accountable for the activity and products of our minds. It also requires us to bring the same kind of rigor to how we interact with the mental activity of others; otherwise, we can inadvertently adopt their ideas and beliefs without examining them. Or we can set ourselves up to be the authorities and experts, thereby accidentally reverting to the external-authority theory.

This is difficult because most of us have so much invested in the dominant system. We have been good students, good teachers, and good at the work we do because we have mastered the game of learning what is required and have been rewarded for it. We are, in other words, satisfied by the answers our methods have produced and the benefits they have delivered to our lives. They are, as often as not, the sources of our livelihoods and identities. Unfortunately, the answers that create satisfaction within the existing system do not begin to address, and may even exacerbate, the complex global issues that human beings must learn to engage with productively. This creates intense inner conflict, as our desire for meaningful change in the world is in direct contradiction to the limitations on our learning and the ways that we get rewarded in life.

As a society and as individuals, to adopt a self-determination theory of knowledge means wrenching ourselves out of our most deeply ingrained patterns, which blind us to the poverty of our approach. This blindness makes it difficult even to discern the connection between the ways we are thinking and learning and the disastrous consequences that are the result. If instead we can let go of our attachments and learn to embrace the uncertainty that this will produce, then we can begin to open the space for deep questioning about the sources of what we claim is true knowledge.

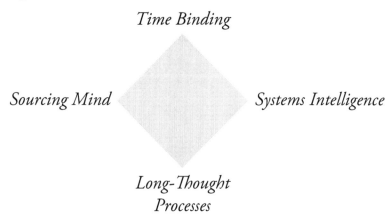

*Time Binding*

*Sourcing Mind*                    *Systems Intelligence*

*Long-Thought*
*Processes*

**Figure 3: Self-Determination Theory of Knowledge Tetrad.**

*Ground*: I have identified the *sourcing mind* as the ground for the self-determination theory of knowledge. This term has several meanings. In the first place, we must constantly remind ourselves to look for the sources of our thoughts and beliefs, rather than accept them unexamined. Then, as we develop our ability to think critically, we will learn to consciously tap into a source of the right nature and order for the work we need to do. Over time, we will gain the experience necessary to bring this source of insight into structured articulation and expression so that it can serve as a basis for our beliefs and ideas.

*Goal*: The goal is *systems intelligence*, the ableness or capability to gain understanding of the innate character and potential of the systems within which we live in reciprocal relationship. Developing this ableness is a demanding practice that begins with dissolving our false belief that each of us is an independent operator rather than a living being arising from and naturally enmeshed with multiple organic whole systems. With fuller awareness, we are able to step into a state of nonattachment and not-already-knowing, which allows us to join with the subject of our inquiry. We are then able to image—to experience with our mind's eye—systems whole and alive, at work with all their aspects and capacities engaged. This way of thinking enables us to discern the essences of entities and systems, which deepens our understanding by peeling back superficial and sensory-based layers of conceptualization and embodying the ways things work.

Finally, as we become anchored in a system's essence, we begin to recognize the in-dwelling potential that it is seeking to realize. Taken as a whole, this process opens the door to a source of intelligence that is beyond personal notions, preferences, or experience. It is a way of harnessing human consciousness to its evolutionary purpose: enabling a living planet to continually manifest more of its potential.

*Direction: Time binding* provides the source of direction, a North Star, for this theory of knowledge. In chapter 3, I introduced time binding as a way to conceptualize the role of humans as conscious enablers of evolution, applying their systems intelligence to regenerating energy fields within which living systems can manifest increasingly more of their potential. The epistemological relevance of the term is that one shifts from knowing to not knowing, aiming to deepen understanding rather than accumulate knowledge. Our North Star is to make a meaningful contribution to collective human wisdom in service to evolution.

*Instrument:* Time binding requires intense devotion to *long-thought processes*, which are fueled by questions of enduring importance. Because conversations around these questions tend to be conducted in clichés, a long-thought process applies conscious effort to dissolve preconceptions and superficial ideas. This enables insight into the essence of the theme or subject around which a question is organized, such as beauty, purpose, ethics, nature, spirit, or meaning.

A long-thought process reminds us to wake up each time we encounter our question in public discourse or inner reflection, saying, *Pay attention! This is the question I'm committed to working with in this moment. My responsibility is to consider what is being said, and through conscious discernment, to deepen my understanding of it and perhaps generate new meaning with regard to it.* This commitment to a question becomes a focus of our efforts to contribute to human wisdom and understanding. When we take it on, we ourselves become a conscious instrument of the time-binding process.

Such a commitment requires us to set aside our earlier thoughts on the subject, which are only one more example of accumulated knowledge, and see it from a new angle and perspective. For instance, in my work as educator, I am committed to never teaching or writing about an idea the same way twice. Each time I am in the role, I reengage with time binding by continuing my long-thought process, discovering new conceptualizations and articulations to deepen my understanding of subjects that I supposedly know a lot about. If I am always starting over, then I can never develop expertise and never take authority over anyone.

The external-authority theory of knowledge demands passive acceptance of the boundaries regarding what constitutes legitimate methods and subjects of inquiry. By contrast, a self-determination theory inherently questions these boundaries, thereby activating far more potential intelligence. One of the effects of this approach is that it encourages people to go back to first principles and dismantle what they thought they knew in order to discover new depths of inquiry. For example, instead of focusing attention on finding a drug to cure a disease, this approach invites us to rethink the nature and origins of the disease and even our assumptions about the concept *disease*. This is how we make breakthroughs in our understanding of the underlying dynamics of life and our universe. It is a sacred wisdom practice, one that we bring ourselves back to again and again so that we come to reflect more perfectly the infinite depth of reality.

# Fourth Intermezzo

I have long made a distinction between *personality*, those characteristics that we adopt to fit in and get along with others, and *essence*, the essential attributes that consistently underlie our choices and the actions we engage in throughout our lives. Personality traits are adaptive and, for the most part, socially conditioned, whereas essence qualities belong to the core of our being. When we move toward essence, intentionally embedding it in what we do and how we do it, we become increasingly authentic in how we relate and distinctive in what we contribute to those around us.

## Capacity-Regenerating Questions: Being

- It may not be obvious at first, but we bring our personalities (our social conditioning) to pretty much everything we do, including our reading. Pause for a moment and reflect on the chapter you just read. Are you aware of your social conditioning as it influences who you are being and therefore how you are relating to the content of your reading?

- Are you also aware of the presence of your essence (it is usually quieter and harder to discern) and how it is relating to the content of your reading? Note: One way to gain a sense of your essence is to reflect on someone who holds you with unconditional caring and love. Who are you in their eyes?

- If you brought your essential self into conscious awareness as you read the next chapter, how would it engage with the content?

# Chapter Five

# No More Gold Stars

When John Watson began developing and promoting his methods a hundred years ago, he explicitly stated his goal: to make behaviorism ubiquitous by embedding it in all our cultural institutions. In particular, he proposed conditioning children from an early age as a way to make this possible. Parenting and the education of young children were especially important arenas to focus on if you wanted to create a population that could be externally controlled.[7]

What is shocking about this is how well it has worked, so much so that, a hundred years later, we have accepted behaviorist conditioning as the completely natural way to organize human affairs. Even those who see themselves as independent or contrarian thinkers often participate unconsciously in the behaviorist approaches invisibly woven into the fabric of contemporary cultures. To change this, we will need to learn to see behaviorism at work in our everyday lives and then uproot and replace it using the self-determination theory of knowledge. Here are two typical examples, beginning with our culturally shared ideas about good parenting.

## Parenting for Self-Determination

Almost all parents seek to raise children with values that will help them thrive and become well-integrated into society. They do so by trying to guide behavior. "Be considerate of others. Share your toys. How would you feel if they did that to you?"

---

7   Kerry W. Buckley, *Mechanical Man: John B. Watson and the Beginnings of Behaviorism* (New York: The Guilford Press, 1989), Kindle edition.

When children model correct behaviors, they are praised: "Good boy! Good girl! Good job!" When they behave inappropriately, they are punished.

Most parents are shocked when I encourage them to stop doing this. "Look," I point out, "you're not teaching her how to think, you're teaching her to do what she's told. She hasn't formed a value within herself; she's only parroted the value that she thinks you want to see." In other words, children look to the most influential person in their environment for guidance about how to think and act. This is usually fine when the kids are young. But what happens when they become teenagers and the most influential people in their lives are their peers?

For parents, the point is to help children think for themselves, but our unconscious adoption of behaviorist methods often undermines this intention. I offer a few suggestions. First, children benefit enormously from witnessing parents and other adults making decisions and choices. As adults interact in a child's presence, they can speak explicitly about what they are doing. "Mom and I are deciding which car to take." Children are naturally mimetic, and this is the kind of learning that they are very good at picking up from their environment. It will provide them with a basis for thinking intelligently about their own choices as they get older.

Second, at some point (often younger than you might expect), children can be engaged with Socratic questioning. For example, a parent might ask a four-year-old on her way to a playdate how she wants to behave toward the other children. Afterward, the parent can invite the child to reflect on how she did and whether she chose the right behavior. Would she want to make a different choice next time?

At first, a child younger than five or six is unlikely to be self-aware enough to answer such questions, but this is a skill that they can quickly develop—choosing how they wish to behave and then monitoring themself for how well they do. In this way, and by making a practice of the Socratic approach, a parent helps them take charge of their own behavior.

Finally, and perhaps most importantly, adults need to stop giving direct instruction about how they want children to behave and stop offering praise and doling out punishment as ways to enforce their instruction. Teaching kids to think for themselves and conditioning them to do what we want are two completely incompatible philosophies of child-rearing, a classic case of mixed messaging. Trying to have it both ways will only confuse children.

These suggestions all work on building a child's capacity to engage with sourcing mind—the ground point in the Self-Determination Theory of Knowledge Tetrad—as they learn to make choices and examine results. The stage is also set for learning systems intelligence, the child's ability to understand the character and the potential of the systems around them, within the familiar contexts of family or classroom.

What these suggestions do not work on directly are the paired ideas of time binding and long-thought processes, which children need to grow into. However, there is one long-thought question that is available to every parent: "What is the unique essence of my child and how do I learn to support them in expressing it as they develop and mature?" Often buried in the unfolding manifestation of a child's essence is a discovery process that will lead them to the long-thought question that will be theirs for the rest of their life.

## EDUCATING FOR SELF-DETERMINATION

I am guessing that most of my readers will remember receiving gold stars from teachers as reward and encouragement. Those who are parents probably still see them on the schoolwork their children bring home. Gold stars are one of a host of techniques that teachers are trained to use to reward children for desired behavior, just as bad grades and detention are among the techniques used to quash undesirable behavior.

Conditioning works best when it is started at an early age, which is one of the reasons behaviorists placed particular attention on parenting and education. The push to design a national system of universally mandated public education offered a highly leveraged opportunity to embed behaviorism in one of society's core institutions. Because children were primarily being trained for positions in the military and industry, it was important to standardize the content they were exposed to and to elicit predictable behaviors. In other words, it was important to take away or severely limit their self-determination and agency. In human beings, especially children, learning is an innate and powerful drive. It expresses itself as curiosity, creativity, and a willingness to spend enormous energies trying to master those things that a given child finds compelling.

But these drives are unruly and idiosyncratic. Children develop at different speeds in different arenas, and their interests are all over the map, placing them at odds with the educational mechanisms we have designed for them. This means that they must be trained to adapt, giving up their own interests and impulses in favor of a collective, standardized enterprise. Thus, we have turned learning, which is inherently natural, fun, thrilling, inspiring, into something rote, oppressive, and even anxiety producing.

Not coincidentally, the need to diminish agency in children was mirrored by a need to diminish the agency of teachers. In a freewheeling environment where children pursue subjects and methods that they have chosen, teachers are equally free to respond creatively, based on the needs and character of each individual child. But in the educational environments that became the norm in the last hundred years, teachers are technicians, implementing standardized lessons to produce standardized results. And, as was inevitable, teachers also are graded and managed, exactly as their students are, with rewards and punishment. Significant deviations from the norm are referred to the professional psychologists on staff in school systems around the country, who administer specialized testing and programs to manage the so-called deviants among both students and faculty.

Perhaps the strongest indication that our present educational system is based on a behaviorist model is the degree to which it requires outside authorities to rank, grade, promote, demote, praise, punish, and correct. Everyone in the system is being told by some authorized and credentialed method of testing that they have either succeeded or failed. Introspection, reflection, and rigorous self-examination are simply irrelevant, and, by extension, so is the ability to think for oneself.

Most of us are products of this system, and much of what I am saying probably is not news, although its origins in behaviorist theory might be. Still, public education is a huge and unwieldy institution, and the many efforts to improve it over the decades have only made these underlying patterns more entrenched. How, then, are we to transform the system into one that can carry out its core function, to raise citizens capable of the intelligent discernment required by a democratic society?

Here are a few concepts for experimenting within and around the edges of the current public school system. One is to connect learning to value-adding activities, which upgrades education from mere knowledge acquisition to engagement in real and dynamic projects in which human action can have impact and consequences. This is an ideal context for developing systems intelligence; complex activities that unfold over time give students a meaningful place to practice holding and working with a long-thought. And because these activities require decision making with real consequences, they also offer students an opportunity to examine and upgrade the sourcing of their ideas. In a living, value-adding activity, it never occurs to kids to ask why they are learning something; it is obvious to them, as they experience themselves becoming more capable and school becoming more exciting and meaningful.

For example, my grandson and several of his classmates set up a chicken coop at their school to produce eggs to share with local families. To do this, they had to learn how to apply for a permit from the city, build a chicken house, raise chickens, and, along the way, overcome multiple challenges large and small. This was a systemic learning process, driven by the students' ideas and interests and their desire to create something of value in the community. It was necessarily characterized by unpredictability, and it required them to be self-managing. Various schools have experimented with programs like this—perhaps the best-known is the Edible Schoolyard Project created in Berkeley by chef Alice Waters—and thus, there are some acceptable precedents for ambitious teachers in conservative schools.

Another practice that can build students' agency and self-determination (and rebuild teachers' and parents') is to invite them to set aims for themselves. These aims provide a basis for self-reflection, helping them to build self-awareness and accountability while growing their ability to assess the effects produced by their choices.

A third and related practice is to eliminate grading and ranking. Children should learn from an early age to set their own goals for their work and to assess accurately how well they do and what they would like to improve. In other words, instead of competing with one another for approval, children thrive when they compete with themselves to get better at what they care about. Teachers are transformed from judges to resources, helping children themselves ask the questions that will guide their natural phases of development. Learning becomes open-ended, ongoing, and self-directed.

By contrast, grading establishes a fixed standard of performance that, once achieved, is the endpoint of learning. Ranking dictates that there is only one place at the top of the heap; all the rest of us must settle for the runners-up positions or learn to think of ourselves as also-rans or utter losers. Grading and ranking imply that we are unable to access our own learning and know best how to move forward and improve; they teach us to depend on expert others to do this for us. No wonder people struggle to think for themselves. They have been told their whole lives that they are naturally incapable and without potential.

Finally, in situations where even these ideas seem impossible to pursue, parents can always help to inoculate their children against the conditioning that schools are designed to deliver. They can, for example, do aim-setting and reflection exercises at home with their kids and encourage them to ask their own questions and develop their own thinking by exploring them. For example, a child might aim to become a good storywriter. With their parents, they could reflect on what, for them, makes a good story and what they would need to do to bring more of these qualities into the stories they write. When children are challenged to think for themselves from an early age, they tend to be more resilient and self-starting students.

Not surprisingly, once behaviorist patterns have been established in childhood, they continue to be replicated in virtually all the rest of our institutions. Businesses, the military, and government bureaucracies all operate from the same assumptions; their authority figures assess our successes, failures, characters, merits, value, scope of responsibilities, suitability for advancement, and so on. This is so prevalent that it does not even occur to us most of the time to question it. It even extends to our personal lives, when we ask for feedback from friends, colleagues, and even customers about how we have done and who we are. It is as if we cannot see ourselves and the effects we have in the world unless someone else gives us the thumbs-up or down.

## SELF-DETERMINATION AT COLGATE SOUTH AFRICA

The Black workers I met during the time I was supporting the change process at Colgate South Africa had been forced to live and work in appalling conditions of coercion and top-down control. For this reason, we were particularly careful not to import European or American ideas about how they should work and what they should work on. I was determined that there would be no gold stars, no patronizing attempts to encourage or model good behavior, in this workplace. Although I did not have a fully developed vocabulary for this at the time, I knew that it would be critical to maintain absolute integrity with a self-determination theory of knowledge. Happily, there was such a pent-up hunger for agency and self-determination within this community that our efforts were received with deep appreciation and creativity.

Working with Black South Africans presented a wide-open field because survival had made them smart and resilient, while apartheid meant that they had almost no exposure to behaviorist practices, education, and institutions. Being asked to be completely self-determining in their thinking and creative work felt natural and joyful to them; they saw my request as an expression of my respect for them as people and the transformative potential that lived in them. The methods, systems, and initiatives that we invented together were informed by Colgate's and my absolute confidence that the workers would rise to any intellectual challenge I put before them, so long as they could see its relevance for their townships and country.

Because our mandate was to grow a new generation of Black leadership from within Colgate's workforce, I did not have to contend with patronizing managers reminding me that these people were uneducated and therefore could not do what I was asking of them. Their response beautifully illustrates the theory of knowledge behind what I did, and this can be mapped against the tetrad that we have been exploring.

**Sourcing mind.** At the time, South Africa was going through an uncertain, turbulent, and even violent transition. As a new leader, Nelson Mandela faced the daunting challenges of dismantling apartheid, creating a new constitution and government, preventing economic collapse, and addressing long-standing conflicts among multiple tribal groups (both Black and White). I knew that if we were to have any chance of succeeding, we needed to ground our work together in a shared, sacred source.

As I interviewed workers from various tribes, it became apparent that they all came from matrilineal societies, where women, especially elders or grandmothers, were the ultimate cultural arbiters. This meant that the metaphor of birthing held powerful shared meaning for them, regardless of tribal origins and even though they were all men. This strong sense of meaning got embedded in our overall claim that we were "birthing a new South Africa," and we invited workers to start every meeting and every event with a story or song that spoke of birthing. It was amazing to see an auditorium of men spontaneously burst into song and dance as our sessions opened, with even the White Afrikaners clapping along. Our work had its source in a powerful and generative archetype, and in stark contrast to the other corporations going through the same transition, we experienced no internal violence at Colgate.

**Systems intelligence.** In contrast to my experience in other parts of the world, these workers had no trouble tapping into the spirit and aliveness of things. This meant that their ableness to engage with systems intelligence was immediate and pervasive. Part of why birthing was such a powerful metaphor for them was that they knew in their bones that they lived in the birthplace of our species. Their origin stories talked about how life called humans into existence to do work on its behalf. Consciousness was a key part of this work because "God speaks to conscious beings." Even in corporate meeting rooms, Colgate workers used song, dance, and ritual to evoke the right mental and energetic states because they knew that ego would separate them from the systems intelligence they sought.

One delightful example of this came when I asked workers to think of diatomaceous earth—a gently abrasive, natural ingredient used as a cleanser in several Colgate products at that time—as something alive that was working with them to create value for their people. They came back from their conversations and danced the life of this fundamental material. Through physical motion, they depicted the ways it might interact with people, and this led them to think of new ways to integrate it into health-promoting products for their families and neighbors. I was moved and impressed by this enlightening expression of kinship with the material world. Through dance and story, they were able to vividly depict the inner workings of a key aspect of Colgate's manufacturing systems and processes, revealing ways that we could upgrade them.

***Time binding.*** Everyone involved in this effort knew that we were working on something big, something that could reweave oral traditions that had been broken or suppressed by colonialism and reestablish the time-binding process of adding to and passing along Indigenous wisdom. After all, the tribes from which these workers came had been living in relationship with the living systems of southern Africa for generations, even millennia. We wanted to find a way to connect the work we were doing as a company to the cultural lineages of place so that the development of consciousness could be reciprocally uplifting and made beneficial for every being that lived there.

To do this, we needed to create a uniting process for bringing our thinking up to a higher order. I proposed to them that this was the way we could accomplish time binding in a single lifetime, even in a single hour. If we could consciously and deliberately evolve the level of our thinking and thereby generate revolutionary, breakthrough ideas, then we could help society take major steps forward.

We decided to transform the way we understood the local cultural and ecological context by engaging in an insight-generating *storying* process. (This, by the way, is how the image of *birthing* became a source and anchor for our work.) We gathered people from within the company, wisdom keepers from the tribes, and scientists from local universities, and together we took a deep dive into the story of the land called South Africa.

Tribal people reminded us that the colonial powers had fragmented and segmented knowledge about this land in a misguided attempt to know everything about it, mostly for the purposes of extracting and exporting its wealth. This had the secondary and perhaps even more destructive effect of fragmenting and belittling Indigenous understandings of place, undermining the cultural beliefs that had enabled people to live in harmony with the South African landscape for eons. Tribal elders, on the other hand, felt that our role should be listening and learning rather than knowing. The task of humans, they pointed out, was to hear, translate, and respond to the voices of plants and animals, winds and rains, earth and sky. This, they believed, was what we all needed to relearn, whether as tribal or colonial people, as individual citizens or corporations. This understanding of the proper role for our species was handed down and elaborated by each subsequent generation; if we tapped back into it, it would anchor our efforts to rebirth the townships, the land, the people, and the nation. It might even help us rebirth Colgate and the industry in which we were embedded.

***Long-thought processes.*** The key to translating all of this into change on the ground was a concept that I named *promises beyond ableness*. Every member of the workforce was encouraged to find an important subject that was relevant to the company's universe and strategy and, at the same time, was something they cared deeply about. It needed to be a subject that they were willing to work on over the coming years. Put another way, each worker identified and pursued his own long-thought process.

In one particularly powerful example, a worker discovered a passionate interest in promoting oral health in the townships. He had interviewed workers on the line producing toothpaste and learned that they and their families all had problems with their teeth and gums. This, he realized, was something he wanted to do something about. He set out to recruit mothers, dentists, educators, biochemists, salespeople, everyone he could think of to help him build a systemic understanding of the oral health problems facing his community and design innovative new programs to address them.

He was using a matrix that I had developed for Colgate, which helped him see the various systems he would need to integrate in order to move his thinking up to a level that would allow him to evolve new insights. The longer he worked in this arena, the deeper his thinking went, and before long, he had become a respected leader or holder of wisdom. Soon, everyone knew to come to him with their ideas and questions about oral health and go-to-market strategies for people in the townships.

The long-standing oral traditions of Colgate's Black workers had given them all they needed for engagement in long-thought processes that resulted in meaningful contributions to their communities. The work we did together to discover a deeper, truer story of the place where they lived had the immediate effect of reigniting their storytelling traditions. Before long, the learning occurring in the context of promises beyond ableness also became stories, entering the oral tradition as contributions to culturally shared knowledge. There was an almost immediate grasp of the relationship between personal research and efforts connected to a subject of inquiry and the larger time-binding work needed to rebirth their country.

In part, the program was successful because we created it to respond to the specific cultural, historical, and business circumstances we encountered at Colgate South Africa. But underlying its design of what we came to call a *noncompetitive contribution hierarchy* were three principles that I have remained committed to throughout my life's work. First, the work design process was created to be strictly noncompetitive. That is, in making a promise beyond ableness, no worker was pitted against another for support or recognition. Each was discovering a distinctive role that he could play and a contribution he could make to the company and to his country.

Second, as part of the work he did in the factory, every worker committed to a professional role related to his promise beyond ableness. By working over a period of years on a subject of importance to customers and the company, each could become a respected leader in his subject area. This went a long way toward supplanting the idea that outside experts were the owners of knowledge.

Third, all workers developed depth of thinking by seeking to understand the essences of what they were working on and of themselves and one another, rather than simply acquiring knowledge about them. This was where hierarchy came in, not as a system of bosses and workers, but as higher orders of contribution that could be achieved by maturing one's grasp of the essences of things. Because of their connection to tribal ways of educating young people, the Black South Africans I worked with were far better at this than workers in any other company I have known. Understanding the essences of entities and systems was their preferred mode of thinking, and they achieved miracles because of it.

# Fifth Intermezzo

I always include stories and case studies when I write because the ideas I am trying to convey cannot be experienced if they cannot be imaged. Stories are a way to cultivate the capability to image in readers, who watch what I describe unfold in their minds' eyes. I am particularly interested in helping readers see the world in terms of *value-adding processes* so that they can develop an understanding of how living phenomena in a living world come into being. A value-adding process view reveals dynamism and effect, rather than static objects.

Let me illustrate what I mean by this. A rudimentary and somewhat solipsistic understanding of value comes from thinking that the object I am making (or service I am providing) is wonderful in itself. This is a *thing view* of value. As I become more sophisticated, I can extend my thinking to consider how the object I am making will attract a potential buyer because I have transformed raw materials into a more useful form and this effort is worth something. This is a *value-added* view. When I arrive at a *value-adding* view, I can image the effect of what I have created as it is being used in the lives of those I have made it for, when they integrate it into their own value-adding processes. The value that I have created comes from the way that I have helped *them* find new ways to create value, which gets passed along to their beneficiaries, and so on in an ongoing chain of value-creation. This multiplication of effects is what makes a process value-adding, but it will remain invisible to me unless I am capable of forming an image in my mind of a system at work.

## Capacity-Regenerating Questions: Being

- Go back and reread any story from the preceding chapters that seemed significant to you. This time, hold the intention to image what is happening in the story as a living, value-adding, value-generating process.

That is, create a multidimensional experience in your mind that considers not only what people are doing but what they are feeling and what is motivating them. Use this mental experience to see the whole of what is happening: how people are relating to one another and to the action of the story, the effects that are being created, and what difference this will make to the larger context within which the story is unfolding. Notice what this imaging creates in you.

- What difference did reading and imaging simultaneously make for you? What changed in the quality of your experience of the content?

- How does this approach expand your understanding of the meaning in what you have read? What will you be able to do with content that you experience this way? How will you extend this practice not only to stories but to all texts?

# CHAPTER SIX

# THE HUMANIST HAZARD

One way to reframe and summarize what I have written so far is that a shift from one theory of knowledge to another reflects a shift from one paradigm to another. The two theories that we have looked at emerge from and reinforce paradigms or ways of experiencing and understanding the world. The external-authority theory of knowledge is perfectly suited to a paradigm that is organized around finding ways to dominate, control, and extract value from ourselves, each other, and the world. Indeed, this theory of knowledge reinforces the paradigm: a person's ability to extract value increases as they move up levels of success and authority.

Over the course of my lifetime, I believe that a much higher order of paradigm has been trying to come back into being. At various times, I have called this a *regenerative* or *living systems* or *evolve capacity* paradigm, and it has always been characterized by a recognition of first principles that are necessary to life and evolution. These principles might be summarized as follows: living entities are naturally whole and imbued with essence; they have unrealized potential that arises from nested interconnections with other systems within fields of structured energy; their potential, which is the driver of evolution, can be realized through inner development.[8] This is a pretty dense description of what I mean by *the regenerative paradigm*, but

---

8    For an in-depth discussion of the first principles of regeneration, see Carol Sanford and Ben Haggard, *Indirect Work: A Regenerative Change Theory for Businesses, Communities, Institutions, and Humans.*

its implication is that each of us humans is also a whole, nested system and always in need of development.

The regenerative paradigm has deep roots. Many people have contributed to or attempted to articulate it, including theoretical physicists (such as David Bohm and Albert Einstein) and a host of ecological thinkers and designers. More important, the regenerative paradigm has long been integral to many Indigenous cultures, influencing their science and lifeways. It also informs those wisdom traditions—some Buddhist and Sufi lineages, for example—that emphasize epistemology, right action, and the development of consciousness. This means that regeneration, despite its current cachet, is neither a flash in the pan nor superficial. It is a venerable paradigm that demands profound and ongoing transformation in our understanding of ourselves and the world and in our thinking and action. This is consistent with a self-determination theory of knowledge.

## HUMANISM

For the sake of clarity and strong contrast, I have so far focused on the difference between the behaviorist approach and a proposed self-directed approach to thinking and learning. However, there is at least one other paradigm, with an associated theory of knowledge, that we should be aware of because it continually muddies the water when we try to get clear about whether we are operating at the regenerative, self-directed level or falling back to a lower level. I refer to it as the *do-good* or *humanist* paradigm.

As a twentieth-century social movement, humanism arose in opposition to the behaviorists. Its roots go back at least to the explorations of eighteenth-century Romanticism and nineteenth- and twentieth-century depth psychology, as well as to European cultures' exposure to oriental philosophies. It gained force in response to the behaviorists' refusal to acknowledge the inner life of human beings as a legitimate concern. This culminated in the social upheavals of the 1960s, which can be understood in part as a humanist repudiation of the mechanistic world that behaviorism has built.

Humanism set out to reclaim the inner lives, the souls, of human beings. As a paradigm, it viewed human creativity, self-expression, and self-discovery as inherently worthy and meaningful, and it celebrated embodied experience, intuition, and feeling. In addition, it set out to reclaim an internal basis for value, recognizing that we can appreciate and benefit from things other than productivity or financial gain. This led to the concept of *values* as something that we can have, individually and collectively. The humanist movement resulted in a proliferation of opportunities for self-actualization by means of everything from spiritual training, psychotherapy, and life coaching to wilderness retreats and corporate mindfulness programs.

## The Hazard

There are two things that particularly concern me about a worldview that is human-centered and focused on self-actualization. First, it invites us to become self-referential, both as individuals and collectively. Whereas a living systems paradigm understands that all beings exist as nested phenomena within reciprocal webs of relationship, humanism focuses almost entirely on the inner experience of individual humans. It views our relationships with other people and with natural systems in terms of their contributions to our welfare and self-expression. We are encouraged to value things in terms of the joy and satisfaction they bring us or the conditions for creativity that they supply. We derive meaning from self-actualization without necessarily considering the larger effects of our attitudes and actions, except in the self-referential sense of assuming that one's own happiness represents a contribution to the net happiness of the world. This results in social atomization and degradation, as we become increasingly able to pursue our lives independently of the life of society, the planet, or the sacred.

Second, seeking to be good people and to be the measures of our own success subtly creates conditions for idealization. Once we have internalized the idea that we have values, it takes only a short step for us to believe that our values are excellent and that, because they make us better people, the world would be a better place if everyone shared them. In other words, we translate something that we esteem into an *ideal* and begin projecting it onto others.

As an outer phenomenon, this becomes destructive when we impose an ideal on someone else, either consciously, by trying to persuade or coerce them, or unconsciously, by simply never considering that they might hold a completely different value. As an inner phenomenon, it becomes self-destructive when we so strongly identify with our ideals that we perceive any challenge to them as a threat. The idealization process can be readily seen in the philanthropic impulse, which is driven by a desire to live out our values and do good in the world. The problem with philanthropy is that it often makes the unwarranted assumption that we know what is good or right to do and that this knowledge can be generalized to diverse situations. The philanthropic impulse very easily turns into a missionary or colonial impulse.

From my point of view, the humanist paradigm is problematic because it can so easily be mistaken for the regenerative paradigm, bleeding off energy that could be used toward life-enabling ends and redirecting it toward self-satisfaction. Instead of pursuing development of the rigorous, disciplined thinking that is required by a self-determination theory of knowledge, it prefers the pleasures delivered by enhanced sensitivity and "finding oneself." Because humanism and doing good are the dominant paradigm for most well-intentioned people (a category that I assume most readers of this book fall into), I want to draw particular attention to how easy it is to take in everything I am saying through a humanist lens.

For example, people regularly say in response to me, "Oh! By self-directing, you mean that we learn to accept everyone as they are and encourage them to do what is in them to do. They are enough just as they are."

"No!" I reply. "That is not what I mean at all." This understanding of self-direction is an existence-based way of thinking. I am talking about what people have *not yet* become, not what they are. I am talking about their potential, based on their essence, for developing and becoming far more than who they have been and contributing far more than they can currently contribute. In a way, *I am encouraging people to let go of their self-definition altogether, replacing certainty about who they are with an ongoing inquiry into what they might serve.* A self-determination theory of knowledge asks us to pay attention to what each of us needs to awaken in ourselves and, in particular, what we need to dedicate ourselves to if we are to undertake our own becoming.

A related source of misunderstanding comes from conflating what I am describing with the relativistic worldview, which accepts everyone's right to their own beliefs and opinions because truth is culturally or contextually determined, never absolute. Relativism arose simultaneously with humanism and has been widely adopted as a humanist concept. As a perspective, it invites us to abandon the discipline of examining ourselves and our thinking processes. This surrender results in failure to understand our conditioning and prevents us from evolving beyond our preexisting biases and attachments. By contrast, the self-determination theory of knowledge emphasizes the dynamism produced by conscious, critical thinking, valuing the evolution of potential over the acceptance of what is.

Like the other theories of knowledge I have explored, humanism has an organizing structure. As the ground from which it proceeds, a humanist theory of knowledge reclaims the value and utility of subjectivity, intuition, and an intrinsic sense of what is good and true. Its goal is well-being and an experience of meaningful connectedness in one's life. It gains direction and creates coherence by framing experience within a metaphysical philosophy, such as Buddhism, mystical or existential Christianity, animism, or the idea that the nature of the universe is love. It uses as its instruments those experiential practices that deliver an altered state of awareness—everything from Gestalt therapy, to breathwork, to meditation, to intense physical exertion, to group encounters, to mind-altering substances used within a ritual context.

At its best, a humanist theory of knowledge enables us to become self-aware and self-observing. We become better able to see ourselves and to recognize the ways that we can be our own worst enemies. This can teach us humility, mindfulness, and compassion for others. These are useful and humanizing qualities, but from a regenerative perspective, they are incomplete; they fail to grasp the meaning of our nestedness in larger living systems and the role humanity plays on Earth. People believe they are good because they are attempting to do no harm. But, when we become aware that our role as humans is an evolutionary one, the insufficiency of minimizing harm becomes blazingly apparent.

At its worst, humanism can enable us to sustain our self-delusions. This is one of the reasons that people become so attached to certain humanist or do-good ideas. So long as we can, through our beliefs and actions, promote a generally accepted image of ourselves as good people, we can avoid the question of whether the good things we are doing are having the slightest effect on what needs to be changed. This is the hazard of accepting and becoming identified with popular definitions of doing good. It invites us to be satisfied with ourselves, rather than to inquire deeply into the contribution that is needed from us and the corresponding self-evolution that we will need to undergo.

Another way of conceptualizing the distinction I am drawing here is to consider the idea that a humanist theory of knowledge focuses on self-actualization, whereas a self-determination theory of knowledge focuses on *systems-actualization*. Systems-actualization starts from the understanding that humans depend for their survival and well-being on their integration into and contribution to living social, ecological, and planetary systems. When we comprehend our nestedness, we recognize that we are by no means separate and autonomous beings; our boundaries relax, and our sense of self extends to encompass those larger systems that interpenetrate psychically and materially with us. Our sense of what is good for us and what is good for the whole merge, and we derive meaning from what we contribute rather than what we gain.

## Human Development

I want to pause for a moment to provide a reminder of why we are investigating this question of how we know what we know. I started *No More Gold Stars* from the premise that the overwhelming and complex problems facing humanity can only be addressed by people who are able to think deeply, creatively, critically, and in a conscious and self-directed way. I also proposed that this ability has been severely compromised by the nearly ubiquitous influence of behaviorism in education, society, and organizations. The problem, I suggested, is one of epistemology. Without an appropriate theory of knowledge, we undermine our own potential—and the potential of those around us—to develop our capacity for the regenerative thinking that is so desperately needed at this time.

Built into the structure of our brains and beings is an innate but undeveloped potential for high-powered, systemic thinking. Unfortunately, the development of this capability is ignored by nearly every process that should be working on it, from parenting to education to apprenticeship and professional development. Instead, these arenas are almost entirely dedicated to behavioral conditioning or, in some cases, humanistic self-discovery, and have adopted methods that condition us to accept only expert-certified content and then disgorge this content in the form of correct answers. High-quality content is, of course, necessary for the functioning of any well-developed mind, but it is without much use if it is not playing its role within a robust thinking and meaning-generating whole.

Humans are born incomplete. Infants are nearly totally dependent and need to develop their ability to walk, speak, and feed themselves. For them to do this in a way that helps them become whole and independent beings, it is important to allow them time and independence to struggle with and overcome increasingly complex challenges. Continually interrupting this necessary process is a good way to instill lack of confidence and agency in a child. In a similar way, our ability to become whole and contributing members of society demands that we develop emotional resilience and a flexible, creative, and self-aware intellect.

Of course, behaviorists recognized that human beings are born incomplete, but they failed to understand this as a state of infinite potential, ripe for development. Instead, they reduced humans to their behaviors and took up the task of conditioning them. Their methods resulted in an orderly and efficient workforce, but even today, these methods continue to cultivate laziness, subordination, and ignorance. Right now, regardless of who we are or where we fit in social hierarchies, we humans simply cannot make our necessary contributions as time binders and participants in the evolutionary work of a living planet. Like a body that never learns to move or to eat nutrient-dense food, we are unable to fully manifest our potential as individuals and as a species.

There is plenty of work to be done to address this lack of attention to true human development, starting with acknowledging and then replacing the beliefs and practices that make us stupid. This will be profound systems change work, for as a system, such as a business, begins to reconfigure its orientation, goals, and purposes away from maintaining the status quo and toward unleashing human intelligence and creativity, it starts to redefine or reconnect to its real potential. As its people grow their intelligence and creativity, they are put to work on evolving the whole of the business. This becomes a virtuous cycle, as the system spirals upward in sophistication, resilience, and innovation. It is precisely what I have witnessed in the businesses I have worked with, and it is hopefully well-demonstrated by my stories about Colgate South Africa.

Human development, in the sense that I am using the term, is hardly a new idea. It has been undertaken in many cultures at many times. For example, in Indigenous communities around the world, development is embedded in rites of passage, especially those that usher children into the world of adulthood. But children are often prepared for years before they undertake these rites, and the following section is an anecdote to illustrate this.

## A Systems-Actualizing Culture

Decades ago, while traveling in Ecuador, I was introduced to an Indigenous woman who was an elder and shaman for her remote community. She was accompanied by a boy, about nine years old, who was assisting her. I was struck by his maturity and quiet composure, and I asked if I could talk with her about this relationship. Through our interpreter, she told me that among her people, It was understood that great-aunts and uncles and other extended family were responsible for the inner development of children. This was to relieve parents, who were occupied with providing for them and giving them a safe environment within which to grow. The role of the great-aunts and uncles was to help children form and test their own thoughts by observing and questioning what was going on around them. The point was not to instruct, but to challenge and to encourage independence. When I asked the elder whether reflection was part of this process, she said, "Yes. That is how we do everything, *especially* with the children."

Another role she described had to do with noticing the calling each child responded to and linking them to someone who could foster it. This was the situation with her grandnephew, the little boy assisting her. He was called to become a shaman. She told me that he was able to be profoundly quiet and to handle complex tasks because he *wanted* to be with her—it was his heartfelt choice—and he knew that it was important not to agitate the spirits. If he could not handle this responsibility, then she could not allow him to stay. Later, when he approached puberty, he would undergo a rite of passage, after which he would continue his tutelage with her until he was prepared to take on the responsibilities of the shamanic role himself.

In what the elder told me, there was no conflict between the development of the boy's inner self and his need to contribute to the well-being of his family, community, and tribe. These values, which are so often in conflict in societies where the external-authority paradigm prevails, were understood to be mutually reinforcing in this Indigenous context.

I believe that in a systems-actualizing society based on the self-determination theory of knowledge, this would be true for all children. Each could become self-determining by choosing and dedicating themself to a necessary role. This is what the shaman was helping me to see when she talked about the developmental relationships between elders and children. The ongoing developmental dialogue that encouraged children to think for themselves from a very early age was how they learned to be self-determining and to recognize and develop their callings—from a young age, knitting themselves into their families and the larger community by making contributions toward its well-being and evolution.

# Sixth Intermezzo

All too often, a person's sense of who they are causes them to stand in their own way when it comes to manifesting more of the potential that is innate in them. For this reason, I encourage people to push the boundaries of who they think they are and what they think they can be. This invites them to step out of their comfort zones and move past what frightens or hinders them. It interrupts the inner voice that says, "I can't do this. It's just too hard!" or "That's not me! I'm not the sort of person who would do such a thing."

When a person lets go of a false self-definition, they can see more possibilities and begin to move toward the self they aspire to be. Life offers unlimited opportunities to take risks, to take on demanding tasks that require personal growth and development. Rather than avoiding these opportunities, we should embrace them!

## Capacity-Regenerating Questions: Being

I encourage you to give some extra time and thought to this set of questions, as your effort here will change the way you engage with content as you read forward.

- Identify an arena in which you are avoiding a call to step up to a different level of challenge, integrity, performance, and consciousness.

- What boundaries—in your self-conception, in your experience, in what you believe you are capable of—do you need to cross to answer this call?

- How can you apply what you have read in this book so far to help you make a change in your being?

# Chapter Seven

# Six Disciplines for Independent Thinking

From an early age, I noticed that I see things that others usually miss. For much of my early life, this was a source of frustration and even pain because I simply could not figure out how to articulate what I was seeing in a form that others could understand or relate to. At times, this made me seem obstreperous, a stubborn child and a difficult woman. I would not budge in terms of what I was and was not willing to go along with. I debated with my teachers and disagreed vociferously with my peers because their premises and reasoning seemed so wrongheaded to me.

It was not until I began to work in South Africa that I understood how a different theory of knowledge was the root of my difficulty and that I could not simply tell people what I was seeing. I needed to create conditions within which they could see for themselves. Those painful early years of irresolvable differences of discernment prompted me to invest a great deal of energy into creating ways for other people to gain access to the self-determination theory of knowledge.

## Six Mental Disciplines

I began by asking myself how we might use the myriad interconnected social institutions that keep the behaviorist paradigm locked in place to move us up to a higher order. This question led me to spend many years articulating a system of frameworks from which to think about the self-determination theory of knowledge. One of these frameworks is a set of six mental disciplines that help guide its application for the development of independent thinking and agency.

The six disciplines fall naturally into two sets of three. The first set has to do with the way we work on our relationships to the world.

> ***Shift Scope of Focus.*** Focus on systems and systems-actualization versus self-actualization or authoritative sources.
>
> ***Orient to Becoming.*** Work with systems in flow as they are *becoming* versus mistaking them for static *beings.*
>
> ***Start from a Whole.*** Root thinking and practice in quantum and Indigenous perspectives versus classical mechanics.

The second set has to do with the way we work on our relationships to ourselves.

> ***Redefine Performance.*** Aim to add value versus extract value.
>
> ***Educate to Express Potential.*** Develop inner capabilities versus reinforce conditioning and stereotyping.
>
> ***Work Indirectly.*** Foster change through inner development versus direct application of force or effort.

These are internal ways of disciplining thought that have everything to do with discerning when we are governing ourselves and when we are not. That is, they enable us from moment to moment to distinguish which theory of knowledge is governing our mentation. They derive from a *regeneration*, or *essence* and *becoming*, worldview that enables us to experience life as whole and dynamic. To think from this perspective requires us to image with our inner eye the working of living systems, to apprehend the weave of their movements and purposes, and to sense the quality of being that threads them together into meaningful wholes.

In my brief descriptions, I have contrasted each discipline with the degraded ways of thinking and knowing that arise when mechanistic and humanist theories of knowledge are in place. These derive from the *existence* worldview that is based on the input of multiple sensory perceptions gathered from material experience. This sensory information is necessarily fragmented and partial, the opposite of systems understanding. Thinking from an existence perspective, without the presence of an inner, imaging eye, can tell us nothing about the invisible patterns that connect phenomena into systems. A worldview based on sensory perception alone leads us to believe that the universe is built of separate, inanimate parts, an infinite clock-work filled with automatons, and we interpret it and our experience accordingly.

The six thinking disciplines are particularly useful in helping us discern not only which paradigm and theory of knowledge we ourselves are operating from, but also what the primary governors are in a situation. They enable us to hear when some-one, including ourselves, is responding unconsciously with a behaviorist attitude. Given how pervasive behaviorism is in our culture, the tendency to improve a situation by managing behavior with rewards and punishments (including their more subtle varieties, such as positive feedback) ends up as the default. We all do this, especially when we are stressed or distracted. In my own case, articulating these disciplines and making them my constant practice sharpens my awareness of this default to behaviorism, and I am able to change my course immediately whenever it occurs.

In this chapter, we will work our way through each of the disciplines.

## SHIFT SCOPE OF FOCUS

With the self-determination theory of knowledge, the appropriate focus is systems-actualization, which can be defined as service to the manifestation of a living system's innate potential and aspiration, and its expression into the world. This is the opposite of visualizing what *we* think this system should and could be: it re-quires us to set aside hubris and attachment to the excellence of our ideas.

We begin to develop our capacity for systems-actualization by imaging the whole of a system and the way it works when it is healthy and operating in harmony with its nature or essence. We explore the ways it relates to other systems and the po-tential contribution it could be making to them. Engaging deeply in this process, without judgment or projection, almost universally has the effect of awakening a sense of respect and caring, and it can foster a desire to help actualize the imaged potential.

It is important to note that this way of engaging a system has nothing to do with identifying and fixing its problems. Once we step into problem-solving mode, we are separated and distanced from the life of the system, back in the humanist world, where we are the heroes of our own stories, doing good *on behalf of* rather than in service to living entities. Or worse, we are in the mechanical world, forcing systems to conform with our beliefs and desires.

In the fully alive world, with a self determination theory of knowledge, our aim should be to help all systems become self-directing. This requires us to subordinate our sense of separate self and seek ways to serve the ability of systems to come into their own. There will always be shortfalls to address and work to be done, but rather than solving problems, our primary job is to listen and learn, and, through this attention, enable the system to direct the ways *it* wants to evolve.

One reason that we in the United States find it hard to accept and practice systems-actualization is that in North America colonization was primarily organized around homesteading. This process depended on an exceptional degree of rugged pioneering individualism, which later became deeply embedded in the national psyche and continues today to be a source of ongoing conflict. We are at odds over the role of society and government in the lives and responsibilities of individuals. Learning to see ourselves as beings who are fully dependent on and in constant exchange with the environments that surround us is one of the educational challenges of our age. You might say that in the United States, the atomization of classical physics has been overlaid and compounded by the cultural emphasis on individualism, making it very difficult to adopt a truly systemic worldview. As a consequence, we typically try to address problems in fragmented and individualistic ways.

For example, think of the proliferation of actions that we are encouraged to undertake toward achieving something called *sustainability*. We recycle water bottles, turn down thermostats, buy organic cotton underwear, and donate to Save the Whales. Notice that all of these are fragmented adjustments to narrowly defined behaviors—best practices, as it were. None of them requires a transformation in how we think, perceive, or participate in the world. None of them will make either us or the world more whole. The alternative is to teach ourselves and our children that we are not atomistic individuals, but living systems nested within other, larger living systems. We need to reclaim the kind of understanding that was universal when all of us operated from an Indigenous perspective, when each of us understood that we were just one being sitting in the circle of life.

I was recently encouraged by an article about a crew of Native American smoke-jumpers who are seeking to employ tribal wisdom about fire as a renewing force in the life of forests and grasslands. Instead of putting fires out reactively, this crew is reclaiming methods for working with fire proactively. They are changing their role from that of crisis managers for forests that are wildly out of balance to contributing participants in forests as living systems. This kind of dedication to serving the well-being of something larger than them does not in any way diminish their individuality or sense of self-worth. Rather, it expands and strengthens a more meaningful sense of self, one that has been redefined in terms of its role within a system. This is precisely what I mean by the shift from self- to system-actualization.

## Orient to Becoming

One condition for playing the game of systems-actualization is the ability to shift or extend our goals beyond achieving personal satisfaction in life. My friend and colleague Charlie Krone, whose work I have often drawn from, makes a distinction between a *being* philosophy of life and a *becoming* philosophy of life. People who operate with the first tend to see life as something that happens, whose ups and downs provide them with opportunities for learning. The primary goal of this journey is the satisfaction of their wants and necessities, including such basic needs as adequate food and shelter, and higher-order aspirations, such as intimate friendship and meaningful work. They expend effort to alter the existing structure of their environment to better serve these ends. Their lives gain richness from the capacity for fulfilling self-expression and a sense of kinship with others, including nonhuman others.

For someone with this orientation, change and growth do occur, but they are not the point. The real goal is to achieve a kind of comfortable stasis, where it becomes possible to rest on one's laurels, secure in the expertise acquired in years of early striving and the prestige, power, and social acceptance that such expertise brings. Many people approach their acquired expertise as a kind of bank account that needs to be filled when they are young and that then can be drawn from later in life. This is why, having reached a certain level of material comfort and social status, they are willing to forgo the effort required to pursue further development and instead enjoy the hard-earned fruits of their labors.

Charlie Krone proposed an alternative orientation. Rather than organizing life around our own satisfaction, we place our attention and effort on the roles we could play in service to something greater than us. We engage and develop our will, using our intelligence and life energy to generate more aliveness in the world and to create new structures—such as businesses, policies, research initiatives, and philos-

ophies—that will produce beneficial outcomes and effects for all. Rather than placing emphasis on satisfying relationships, we focus on the continual evolution of the
self in order to grow into the contributive roles we feel called to play.

Of course, these different values do not necessarily have to be in conflict. Once
we have committed ourselves to *becoming*, the accomplishments and vicissitudes of
*being* offer unlimited raw material for development. For example, there is no inherent contradiction between being a good parent and householder and doing this in
a way that grows one's ability to serve the manifestation of potential in one's family,
neighbors, and fellow citizens.

These two philosophies have very different origins. Orientation to *being* comes
from deeply ingrained attitudes about what constitutes a good life, attitudes that
are transmitted by our families and societies. Orientation to *becoming* comes from
what I think of as a sacred source, one outside of ordinary material concerns,
plugged into the nature of life itself. This source cannot be readily transmitted; it
needs to be committed to and worked for and becomes stronger in our lives as a
result. The more we are willing to commit to the inner promptings of becoming,
the more our capacity grows and the more it becomes stabilized as a core factor in
our lives. This stability gives us access to the energy needed to work on systems-actualization and the long-thought processes that enable us to take on our role within
the global system of life.

## Start from a Whole

For a long time now, the generally accepted assumption has been that reliable and
verifiable knowledge can only be generated through rigorous application of the
scientific method. This method establishes knowledge by proving or disproving
hypotheses in controlled and replicable experiments. In practice, this has required
isolating objects so that they can be studied with a minimum of complication
caused by uncontrolled influences (otherwise known as controlling the variables).
The result is a mechanical science—antagonistic to the complexity, relatedness, and
structured interconnectivity of living systems—which has yielded a vast body of
knowledge comprising oversimplified and decontextualized fragments.

Any number of critical problems arise from this intellectual mechanism. For
example, industrialized agriculture has been based on the idea that plant growth
depends on a limited and knowable list of nutrients and that soil is an inert medi-

um into which controlled doses of these nutrients can be introduced. The initial gains in productivity that came from thinking of farms as factories have exacted devastating long-term costs and resulted in a global food system that is increasingly precarious as it becomes increasingly simplified.

Acting as though soils are dead has led to dead soils, and acting as though plants are nutrient-metabolizing machines has led to plants that are nutrient poor and prone to disease or predation. Soils and plants are alive, complex, adaptive, and in continuous exchange with the environmental dynamics of weather, climate, carbon cycling, pollination ecology, evolving predator populations, and so on. In other words, the variables cannot be controlled. A nonindustrial, living agriculture needs to draw from a non-reductionist, living science.

One of the fallacies of mechanical science is the notion of the objective observer, empty of preconception and arm's length from the phenomena they are observing. Physicists have come to understand that, at a subatomic level, the mere act of observing will exert an influence on its result. This is also true at the macro level. By endeavoring to adopt an infallibly objective stance, we kill or denature the things we want to study.

The scientific traditions of many Indigenous peoples take an opposite stance—they put the observer into the system as a member of the circle of life and as a child of the forces that create everything. From this perspective, the phenomena we study are kindred. They are made of the same stuff as us and operate according to the same principles and laws. We can know them both objectively, as autonomous and differentiated beings, and subjectively, as woven into the same connecting tissue that we are and therefore imbued, like us, with a common nature. Thus, to know something requires not isolating it, but rather being with it in an attitude of respect and attempted understanding.

Here is an example of what I mean. For some years, Regenesis Group has been evolving a practice that they call Story of Place◊. Its purpose is to understand a specific socioecological system—a bioregion, for example—as a whole and coherent entity with a distinctive nature, or essence, and a valued contribution it could be making to larger social and ecological systems. This understanding informs a range of endeavors, such as creating strategies for economic development, managing the interactions among people and local forests or rivers or coastlines, planning new infrastructures, and fostering viable and life-enhancing businesses.

Story of Place takes an approach completely different from that taken by such current practices as environmental impact studies. These assemble multiple bodies of fragmented information, provided by experts and organized together based on a legally determined template. Sometimes this information is correlated or cross-referenced, but it is never intended to evoke the image of an ecosystem as a living whole.

By contrast, Story of Place starts from a living whole, a place. The researcher brings an alert and open mind, seeking to discover a layered and evolving narrative. They form a dynamic mental image of the place as a living entity engaged in processing the energies (geological, hydrological, climatological, biological, historical, economic, etcetera) that contribute to who it is. The story grows by adopting multiple points of view, and each new perspective gets woven into the image of the whole, shedding light on and deepening understanding of how it works.

At some point in the compilation of the story, an attentive observer will begin to see core patterns connected to the essence nature of the place—the source of those differences that any visitor can feel among, for example, Manhattan, Mexico City, and Paris. These core patterns are overlooked in virtually every modern planning process, yet, when understood, they reveal precisely those qualities that enable a place to offer something of distinctive value to the world, and therefore, they form a basis for a viable economic, social, and ecological future.

I propose that this storying approach is a more truly scientific way to make sense of a socioecological system than the slicing and dicing that makes up a standard environmental assessment—if, that is, we can agree that the purpose of science is to help us gain deep insight into the living nature of things and how they work. Story of Place helps us understand systems that are complex, layered, dynamic, and very much alive, in much the same way that observing live frogs in their living swampy context is preferable to dissecting them on a lab tray—when understanding their aliveness is our aim.

## REDEFINE PERFORMANCE

Modern society has produced a *me culture* that encourages us to assess our choices in terms of *what's in it for me*, our relationships in terms of *putting me first*, and our accomplishments in terms of *the recognition I deserve*. This reflects an underlying societal conviction that life is about extracting value and that all species compete in a zero-sum game for the relatively limited resources available on the planet. By contrast, I hold that life is value-adding and that all species secure their places within ecosystems by making contributions to evolving the whole.

We humans do this by benefiting the lives of specific people and living systems and learning to track and upgrade the downstream effects that our actions have on those we are committed to serving. We become engaged in value-adding processes when we invest direct effort connected to our life's work, when we have specific beneficiaries in mind, and when our efforts are of clear value to these beneficiaries because they address their essence-based aspirations.

Learning to think about downstream effects is not particularly difficult, but because it is neglected in our parenting and educational systems, it rarely shows up in the conduct of our lives or work. Instead, we teach children and young people to seek self-satisfaction, attract the good opinion of others, and pursue learning that will guarantee future earning power. In the process, we grow value-extracting adults while suppressing young people's basic desires to contribute to and care for others.

These different approaches to life lead to very different ways of evaluating performance. Do we calculate success based on how much others admire us or how well we have met our own expectations? Or do we use a far more demanding test, namely the degree to which our efforts on behalf of others have enabled them to close the gaps that prevented them from pursuing their own value-adding processes?

## EDUCATE TO EXPRESS POTENTIAL

We operate in a society that assumes that the shape of a person's character and potential are determined at birth. We may be unconscious of this, but we give ourselves away whenever we say, "Oh, that's just how so-and-so is. They've always been that way. They're a *Scorpio*, you know." Or, if not a Scorpio, then an introvert, or an Enneagram Four, or on the autism spectrum, or possessing a high IQ, or whatever the preferred system of classification might be. These pigeonholes are ways of saying that people have certain fixed and immutable characteristics, the drivers of who they are and what they will be suitable for and capable of in life. From them, we infer that we can give people skills and provide them with opportunities, but the scope of what they will be able to accomplish is narrowly defined by the innate capacity they were born with.

This assumption is pervasive and built into the theories and methods of social science. Our systems of education, psychological testing, career tracking, and advancement are based on the need to separate wheat from chaff. We believe, whether we are conscious of it or not, that people should be sorted and appropriately slotted according to their merit, aptitude, and the relative quality of their minds or bodies. Even when we object to the outcomes of this approach, we usually do so on the basis that they are unfair and promote inequality. Such arguments only serve to reinforce the underlying, unconscious agreement that people were born a certain way and should not be punished or rewarded for it.

I hold that all humans are born with open-ended potential and that the scope of what they can take on in life is unlimited when this potential is developed. Put another way, we are born incomplete and are given a human lifetime to grow ourselves into what we have potential to become. This growth can be accelerated or retarded based on whether those around us recognize and commit to its importance. The real tragedy of our current social systems is that human development is ignored because it is assumed to be irrelevant.

In the self-determination theory of knowledge, development is a lifelong process, something that we do for ourselves and help others do for themselves in response to the commitments we take on and the challenges life puts before us. I can see at least three contexts within which we are called to develop. First are the curveballs that we encounter in life, such as the unexpected death of a friend, a family member's disability, an ongoing conflict with a work colleague, or an exciting but scary new career opportunity. Each of these situations offers the possibility to transform the person we are able to be and the wisdom we can bring to the roles we play, but to do so, we must consciously accept the invitation to develop ourselves.

Second, development can be grounded in evolving our ability to actualize the systems that we work within—in other words, in creating our own learning path based on things that we care about and that clearly need our participation. For example, many people report that their single most powerful motivation to grow themselves comes from their desire to support the healthy development of their children. When we care enough about something, we become willing to get over ourselves and get on with figuring out how to supply what is actually needed.

Third, development can be driven by a global imperative, a sense of lifelong vocation, which, when we are awake to it, weaves together the many things we have chosen to take on. This is very closely connected to our essences, who we are as individuals. It is also what is behind the idea of a long-thought question. When a global imperative has been activated in us, we cannot escape the knowledge that we are taking on something huge, we are in over our heads, and we are going to need to keep growing our capacity for understanding as long as we live. This is probably the most direct way to bring meaning into our lives, and development is at its core.

## Work Indirectly

John Watson, the founder of behaviorism, drew heavily on the thinking of Isaac Newton, including classical mechanics, when he insisted that the only way to influence and manage human beings was to apply direct pressure on them. Consciousness, from Watson's perspective, was a fairy tale; it could not be directly observed, and therefore it did not exist. In his view, both the material and the human world could only be shaped by direct action, not by inner development.[9]

This bias has shaped every aspect of how the world has come to regulate its affairs and respond to its problems. If there is famine, send food. If people need to know something, tell them. If traffic is too slow, widen the freeway. If traffic is too fast, increase the number of speeding tickets. If carbon dioxide is overwhelming the atmosphere, then disinvest in fossil fuels and reinvest in solar. When you find a solution that works, scale it up like crazy. This approach is targeted and measurable, and it results in continuous fragmentation in both action and thought, along with a corresponding inability to understand, let alone anticipate, systemic consequences.

One way to characterize our current situation is that the world is operating with a mechanistic theory of change based on the idea of direct work. If you want to change a system, you must figure out what is wrong with it and then fix it. Find the weak links, analyze the problems, look for points of leverage where relatively small investments will create big changes, then replicate to scale. If the systems that manage the systems are not addressing changes that are needed, then put direct pressure on them, too. Start letter-writing campaigns, take to the streets, advocate in Congress and on the airwaves and in voting booths. Even among systems thinkers, this mechanistic and materialist approach is the norm because generally, they are thinking about systems as machines.

---

9    Kerry W. Buckley, *Mechanical Man: John B. Watson and the Beginnings of Behaviorism* (New York: The Guilford Press, 1989), Kindle edition.

I propose a very different theory of change based on the idea of indirect work.[10] In an indirect approach, the development of consciousness is central, along with the development of culture and capability. Whereas existing theories of change are dedicated to whacking every mole, the indirect theory acknowledges that the most powerful places to intervene lie far upstream in the initial formation of choices about which actions to pursue and why. An indirect approach emphasizes self-management and self-determination, caring, depth of understanding, ability to anticipate systemic effects, and dedication to serving the evolution of something beyond oneself. When these changes begin to occur within individuals, communities, and nations, a field of creativity opens. Actions are conceived and chosen within a potential space, rather than a problem space. Direct work addresses existence, which means that it is primarily about maintaining a status quo. Indirect work addresses evolution.

---

10 Carol Sanford with Ben Haggard, *Indirect Work: A Regenerative Change Theory for Businesses, Communities, Institutions and Humans.*

# Seventh Intermezzo

Self-development is always an option, from childhood through adulthood to elderhood. Developing oneself involves learning to self-manage motivation—or, to put it another way, developing will and personal agency. These give us the basis for evolving our being and function in service to the things we most care about.

As we mature, we pass through recognizable stages of development, each with its own kind of motivation: self-satisfaction, social-satisfaction, ego management, self-actualization, and systems-actualization. As young children, we direct our will toward satisfying ourselves, and this builds the confidence we need to progress to later stages. We then begin to focus on fitting in to our social environments. At some point, we learn to manage our ego, which sets the stage for actualizing ourselves as whole beings. Under the right conditions, we become fully mature and commit to actualizing the potential in something larger than us.

## Capacity-Regenerating Questions: Will

- Test this idea of stages of development and evolution of motivation by looking at your own life. Which kinds of motivation have shown up for you, and at what times? What changed when you passed from one stage to the next? How were these changes reflected in your will and personal agency?

- What difference does it make to bring consciousness to these shifts? How might this serve your capacity to manage your own motivation?

- With regard to this book, if your aim were capability to sustain a higher level of motivation as you engage with it, what would your will need to connect to? What larger purpose would enable you to maintain consciousness of this aim? What does this suggest about how you might approach other books or forms of communication in the future?

# CHAPTER EIGHT

# SELF-DIRECTED THINKING AT COLGATE SOUTH AFRICA

My framework of six mental disciplines emerged during the extraordinary three and a half years I spent with Colgate South Africa in the 1990s. We knew going into this situation that we did not want to use the conventional management tools that the corporation was using elsewhere in the world. Colgate maintained discipline through an organizational hierarchy that specified chains of command and the delegation of work. Its employee handbook laid out expectations and rules of conduct, along with rewards and punishments. We aimed to supplant these methods by growing a culture of self-discipline. And out of this intention grew my framework, which was translated into drawings by employees and taped up on the walls of every meeting room.

## SHIFT SCOPE OF FOCUS

We set out immediately to shift focus from *self* to *system*. Right at the outset, the general manager, Stelios Tsezos, set the tone and direction when, in an address to all company employees, he promised that what we were undertaking was to build a great country while building a great company. He went on to say that we were not afraid of the new constitutional mandate that leadership must represent the racial diversity of South Africa; we *embraced* it. Everyone would become leaders in what we were setting out to do, and the many perspectives within the multiethnic workforce would be incorporated into both the learning processes we would undertake and the strategic decisions we would need to make.

A systems focus permeated everything we did. One illustrative example had to do with how we measured performance. We no longer evaluated people as individuals. Instead, we had teams evaluate their own performances based on the differences they were making for customers. The company adopted a set of external measures based on what customers and consumers considered important, using them in place of the internal measures (such as quantity of product shipped) that had been used in the past. The teams then looked for places in our design, production, sales, and other business processes where they could innovate to address these customer-based measures. Whenever we moved the dial in a significant way regarding some measure that was important to our customers or their businesses, we held a celebration to acknowledge our collective success.

## ORIENT TO BECOMING

One of the revolutionary concepts we pioneered at Colgate South Africa was a *noncompetitive contribution hierarchy*. This was organized around a matrix of increasingly challenging and complex arenas, in which initiatives could be undertaken for the purpose of evolving the company's overall effectiveness. We eliminated competition for position and pay and replaced it with the requirement that every individual create initiatives to evolve the company's performance vis-à-vis its customers. These initiatives needed to meet several critical criteria: demonstrably advance the overall corporate strategy and direction; be relevant to the specific market or customer group that they were intended to address; contribute to the company's financial health; and innovate a way to help Colgate South Africa go beyond what we were currently doing or even capable of doing.

This new requirement shifted people's orientation from being (defining themselves by their position, compensation, and past accomplishments) to becoming (making promises beyond ableness and growing capability to serve the evolution of their customers). The initiatives they chose for themselves were by definition a stretch because they were aimed at moving us all beyond the status quo. In other words, just as workers were becoming more of what was needed in that time and place, so was the company.

Part of what made this so compelling was that we moved from a hierarchy of control to a hierarchy of effects. Workers committed themselves to making a difference to some customer or user and developed an idea for how to make it happen. They were supported by a team that was deeply familiar with the overall company strategy and could help them evaluate and upgrade their plan until it had a high likelihood of success. Based on this, they were able to negotiate an increase in their compensation in proportion to the financial improvement that was generated by their initiative.

The company placed no arbitrary ceilings (e.g., based on race, rank, or educational status) on employees' ability to progress. On the contrary, each individual was encouraged to take on increasingly significant challenges as they gained experience and confidence. This shift in orientation from *me* to *my customers* had a profound effect on the corporate culture; competing with one another no longer made sense. Everyone became agents of evolution—for themselves, the company, their customers, and their communities—and Colgate South Africa became a will-based organization with the internal capacity to do the impossible.

## START FROM A WHOLE

Prior to this time, Colgate South Africa had followed conventional corporate practice when it came to management and employee evaluation. Employees were assigned responsibility for fragments of work activity, such as minimizing waste or maximizing on-time delivery, and annual performance reviews were based on improvements to these fragments. This approach reflected the method and worldview of mechanistic science, breaking complex living processes down into simplified fragments for the purpose of making them easier to manage.

From the outset, we disrupted this process by asking each employee to take responsibility for making life better for some living whole—a customer, user, distributor, or other Colgate stakeholder. Finding ways to participate in and contribute to the self-directed activities of a living entity evoked a whole-systems way of thinking on the part of employees. You might say that they were operating within the laws of a living or Indigenous science. They became increasingly able to recognize and address the multiple forces, relationships, and changing dynamics that provided a context for this entity's efforts—to work with it as a living system.

The results were groundbreaking initiatives that were flexible and sophisticated responses to local conditions. Whole-systems thinking also shifted the relationship of the company to Black South Africans, who had good reason to distrust large corporations. For the first time, they experienced a company that was exercising its power *for* them rather than *over* them.

This approach also included treating each worker as a whole being, and workers began to treat one another in the same way. Each of these men was so much more than his job title, background, or tribal affiliation. He was a dynamic being with open-ended potential, creativity he could discover, and agency he could tap. Taking responsibility for and caring about the well-being of a specific customer drew on the whole of his experience as both an individual and a South African and demanded that he develop the capabilities he would need to rise to the occasion.

This very quickly began to show up as a cultural influence. Within the company, we saw an immediate cessation of intertribal conflict, and this began to communicate outward into the townships where Colgate employees lived. One man described taking on responsibility for a living whole as a new rite of passage—instead of proving one's manhood by killing someone or something, workers were proving themselves by making life better for the people of their communities.

## Redefine Performance

In many companies, superiors evaluate the performance of individual workers based on internal measures related to tasks and deliverables. At best, this drives workers to think about how to increase efficiency and the amount of value that can be extracted by doing good work. At worst, it drives them to devote energy to protecting their benefits or competing with colleagues for recognition. In neither case is the customer considered, and, more often than not, performance reviews end up killing worker spirit.

At Colgate South Africa, evaluation was built into the design of projects based on employees' promises beyond ableness. To secure the support of the company, workers teamed up with developmental *resources*, people within the company (often former supervisors) who had chosen to take on the new role of resource to workers who were developing their capacity. Together, worker and resource created the plan for a project based on a promise beyond ableness, laying out the commitment in explicit terms: what the project intended to do, the beneficial effects it aimed to produce for a specific market or customer, the contributions it would make to Colgate's financial performance, who would need to be involved and the kinds of capabilities they would need to develop, how all of these things would be measured, and how corresponding course corrections would be made along the way. The process was transparent and worker-led, and by the end of a project, the evaluation was self-evident to pretty much everyone involved.

## Educate to Express Potential

Workforce development tends to follow the same behaviorist model that guides public (and most private) schools. Education is seen as a conditioning process by which workers are trained in a predetermined set of skills, following a generic curriculum, for the purpose of generating relatively predictable and manageable patterns of competency and behavior. Often, career progression is linked to the number and level of training programs that a worker has undergone and, by extension, the amount of conditioning that they have internalized.

The self-determination theory of knowledge, which was what we were attempting to work from in South Africa, replaces the generic content and methods of behaviorist training. It teaches people how to use living systems frameworks within a developmental process directed toward manifesting and evolving potential. The frameworks build people's capability to manage their own thinking, find and address the gaps in their understanding, and release their conditioned attachments to old ideas in order to generate innovative insights and concepts. The developmental process anchors this learning by building people's capacity to reflect on their own thinking and to test it against the premises they hold about how the world works and their lived experience of what happens when their thinking evolves.

At Colgate South Africa, we developed a structured ritual: the core team gathered every six to eight weeks for a three- to four-day workshop that ultimately touched every person in the company. People on the core team would later extend the developmental work they had undertaken by engaging their natural work teams to evolve processes for delivering increasing benefits to customers and securing the future of the company.

The workshops were not trainings, with an expert at the front of the room delivering answers and techniques to the participants. On the contrary, they were intensive capacity-development sessions. I would introduce frameworks to the core team that could be used to structure inquiry. Their teams would later use these frameworks to generate and explore relevant questions concerning ways to evolve the value generated by the work for which they were responsible. Finally, they would test their answers, first by reflecting on their process and the expected effects that their ideas would produce for customers, then by acting on them and reflecting (often with participation from these customers) on the effects that were actually produced.

As a result, workers from across the company rapidly expanded their ability to think about business and act as work leaders. They were all learning to think like CEOs. This meant that they no longer required supervisors, and the people who had filled supervisory roles could move into more productive and developmental activities. It also meant that we were seeding an entire population of leaders who could take up vital roles within a changing nation.

## WORK INDIRECTLY

The lingering influence of mechanical physics is evident whenever people set out to change something. They operate from the assumption that change requires working directly on the thing to be changed. One begins by identifying the change to be made, then sets one's goals, breaks the problem down into its component parts, prioritizes what to work on, isolates the variables, identifies a targeted intervention, takes action, course corrects, and evaluates the results. What gets overlooked in this approach is the effect of fragmenting and simplifying complex living processes, which almost inevitably leads to unintended consequences and sets the stage for the next fragmenting change effort.

To abandon this way of thinking and working required a leap of faith on the part of Colgate South Africa. They had been a conventional corporation, accustomed to the fragmenting approach practiced almost universally in the corporate world. In other words, they looked at things that they could measure and ignored or discounted things they could not. We turned that approach upside down, insisting that we needed to teach people to look at living wholes and systemic effects.

The company was a living whole, and it was nested within living wholes—the communities and the society surrounding it. If we wanted to evolve the value we could produce, we needed to understand its value within the life and health of those communities and that society. This meant that we needed to learn to anticipate and track qualitative differences occurring within these systems, differences that would allow them to become more of what they aspired to be. This evolution in value would be reflected in revenue growth, but one would not be able to see it by looking at revenue alone.

The projects that workers were taking on, their promises beyond ableness, served as nodal interventions within these larger systems. For example, when one group focused on improving dental health among children in the townships, they already knew from their own experience that this would have a ripple effect on the well-being and prosperity of the children's families. This understanding was built into the design of every promise beyond ableness. By improving life for one customer or user, we were aiming to grow potential across the whole system.

But this required deep understanding of the life of this customer, including the thwarted aspirations that they were striving to fulfill and their relationships to the larger systems within which they were embedded. To create this understanding, we taught workers to generate images of who they had chosen to serve, bringing them to life in their minds as whole beings. We were working with people whose Indigenous ways of learning had not been much influenced by Western education, and thus they already knew how to image whole beings. It was just a matter of opportunity—getting to use this capacity to understand their customers within their contexts.

Our strategy turned the company around in a matter of months. When I arrived, the shocks accompanying the end of apartheid were causing the company to lose money. By the end of the first year, we were seeing revenue growth of 35 percent. At the end of the second year, 39 percent. By the end of the third year, 45 percent. You could have found any number of direct and indirect results to measure if you went looking for them—improvements in hygiene, health, and knowledge about self-care; reductions in stress and violence. But we would never have produced these results if these were the things that we had chosen to pursue and measure. We got them because we were working on transforming the sense of well-being, purpose, hope, and potential within an entire society, using the products and services we had at our disposal. We were able to do this because we were working indirectly with the people inside the company (as well as with external stakeholders who got swept up by the excitement around what we were doing) to grow capability, community culture, and consciousness. These gave them exactly what they needed to *be the change they wanted to see.*

# Eighth Intermezzo

As we develop will, moving motivation up to the systems-actualizing level, we become able to commit ourselves to causes beyond ourselves. We mature from willfulness to willingness, as our choices become guided not by ego but by the desire to serve what is alive and meaningful to us. We can develop this receptivity in ourselves by thinking about three distinct *lines of work*.

At the third line of work, we ask ourselves what the purposes and meanings of our actions are. How are they intended to serve the evolution of the community or system that we are dedicated to serving? At the first line, we ask how we will need to develop ourselves if we are truly to serve this purpose. At the second line, located between ourselves and the larger system, we ask what quality of relationship with others we will need to grow if we are to fulfill our purpose.

## Capacity-Regenerating Questions: Will

- I hope that as you read this book you are thinking about specific arenas where you can apply what you are learning. Making it concrete in this way gives the ideas meaning and power and allows you to test their validity in your own experience. Given this, what is an arena or system that you care about and would like to apply your learnings to? (You may wish to refer to the sixth intermezzo for some possible clues.) What purpose are you pursuing with regard to evolving the potential of this arena?

- What will you need to develop in yourself to be more effective and to shift to a self-directed way of working? How can what you are reading here be applied to this purpose?

- Who are you going to engage with in your work, and how are you going to relate to them to achieve the contribution that you intend to make?

# CHAPTER NINE

# DEVELOPMENTAL PRACTICES

I know from long years of experience with groups and companies around the world that the self-determination theory of knowledge works. It creates extraordinary results in the real world. What happened at Colgate South Africa was exemplary, in large part because so many of the workers there had not been conditioned to seek an outside expert to solve their problems for them. But even here in the United States, where behaviorism has been conceptualized, systematized, and spread into every aspect of society, I have seen people liberate themselves from their educations and socially sanctioned identities to do powerful and transformational work.

This does not happen on its own. It requires thoughtful, concerted effort to build and sustain deep change inside of people. This also works best within the context of a value-adding process, where some group (usually a business) is trying to evolve its contribution to people, communities, and the world. Within this context, people have the motivation and working relationships that make it easier to do the hard work that is required.

There are three primary conditions to be met when a business seeks to tap into the energy, creativity, and will to serve that management based on the self-determination theory of knowledge unleashes. First, it must adopt a strategy of the whole, directed toward the evolution of wholes. By this I mean that the business must commit itself to pursuits that will evolve the value it will deliver into a bounded set of markets that it has identified for itself. These pursuits should be so challenging and compelling that they self-evidently require the energy and intelligence of everyone in the business to pull them off. To grow an innovative, self-directed culture is not to create a free-for-all. On the contrary, this work requires focus, discipline, and alignment of effort. This becomes possible only when everyone sees themself as a member of the whole—which has consciously charted a specific direction for itself—and thus can translate its pursuits into meaningful promises that will enable them to contribute to the lives and aspirations of those they serve.

The second requirement is a radically new work design, one that replaces toxic systems and practices with those that support the growth of self-directing people. By *work design*, I mean the structures that determine how people are hired, managed, promoted, and organized to carry out their day-to-day tasks. In most businesses, work design is behaviorist in orientation: hierarchical, competitive, and driven by expert opinion. None of these foster a self-determination theory of knowledge.

What is needed are structures that evoke personal agency within a noncompetitive hierarchy of contribution, based on understanding what customers care deeply about and dedicating oneself to finding ways to assist them toward fulfillment of their aspirations. All of this must fall within and be directed by a strategy of the whole. As we demonstrated at Colgate South Africa, this kind of work design unleashes powerful energies as workers connect their self-development to creating a difference.

The third requirement is to recognize that none of this will work without focused and ongoing development of capability, consciousness, and a community culture. The self-determination theory of knowledge centers on our capacity to become increasingly able to motivate and govern ourselves by continually examining and deepening our own thinking. This is a lifelong process, but not, as it is sometimes described, one of lifelong learning. Learning has to do with knowledge accumulation, while development has to do with the layering and deepening processes associated with growing wisdom.

Wisdom requires us to shed what we think we know, along with our attachments and the positions we hold, defend, and identify with. This is why I connect development to long-thought processes, which require us to shift and intensify our relationships to profound questions over a lifetime. Development, in other words, works not just on what we are able to do, but also on who we are able to be and the commitments we are therefore able to keep.

Unfortunately, development is hard to sustain. This is why I always think of it as a community-related process. Communities like the one we formed within Colgate

South Africa are able to build cultures and energy fields within which development can readily occur. Otherwise, it is easy to fall off the wagon and become complacent about our intentions, losing sight of the real work it takes to live up to them—and communities can fail, of course, if they lack conscious purpose and intention or come under the sway of authoritarian leaders. A developmental community finds ways to disrupt dogmatic certainties by creating rituals that invite people to examine how they are thinking about and working on things. It also supplies them with peers who are a little farther along the path, peers who can help them recognize their own blind spots and maintain the will needed to direct their own developmental efforts.

## Capability Development

I would like to go deeper into what I mean by *capability building* and why I think it is so important. I start from a basic premise that we humans, myself very much included, are works in progress. At the individual, national, and species level, we have the potential and the imperative to evolve who we are and how we think and act. We are not meant to be locked into lazy and destructive habits. We, every one of us, are defined by our ability to have new realizations, to push our minds and beings into new territories, and to place this unique capacity to work in service of life on our planet. As I have argued before, this is our evolutionary role; this is how we earn our keep on Earth. Self-centeredness, nationalism, speciesism—these are just indicators of arrested development, the unsurprising results of an anti-developmental culture that accepts without question the inevitability of top-down, expertise-driven systems.

The need to awaken the inner hunger for self-directed development in people and communities, to counteract the tendency toward mechanicalness, is urgent and requires our most serious attention. I believe it is the only life-affirming way out of the current existential crisis facing our species. In the four chapters that follow this one, I offer a set of developmental practices that are "road-tested" to be highly effective means for doing this work. This is because they are anti-behaviorist by design and are intended to shake us up and wake us up, breaking through our habits of mechanicalness. They come out of a coherent technology and hang together as a coherent approach. For this reason, I want to caution against cherry-picking the practices that seem most appealing or easiest to implement in your circumstances. The practices need to be taken up as a whole, as a way of making the six disciplines for independent thinking (introduced in chapter 7) a way of life.

## SHAKE UP AND WAKE UP

The reader may have noticed a subtle pattern in what I am unfolding here: I keep redirecting attention from *what* we should be doing to *how* we should be doing the things we are doing. This places me at odds with the majority of corporate training practices, educational methodologies, and environmental or social advocacy efforts. Instructing or conditioning people to do the right things (best practices, socially aware speech, and so on) has very little effect on who they are and who they can become. It does not evolve their will or their being, let alone their ability to examine and evolve their beliefs and thought patterns. If anything, it encourages people to stay in their existing patterns, while it substitutes one set of content for another.

Waking people up—engaging their critical thinking, caring, and capacity for taking on complexity—requires something very different: challenging ourselves and one another to question assumptions and bring a new way of looking at things every time we go to work. This becomes a life practice, a way of being in the world, and it very quickly begins to build a culture within which people *expect* to be awake.

Just to be clear, I am not saying that we do not work on content or that content does not matter. We still have real work to do, customers to serve, a society that needs improving, and children that must be fed. My point is that *we can do this work asleep or awake*, and if we choose to be awake, to be present and intentional about our doing, then we must commit to continually examining and evolving the way we work—and the way we think about work—every time we do it. This is why I emphasize questioning beliefs and assumptions. How are we to avoid complacency about things that seem to be going pretty well (or to change recurring patterns that aren't) if we do not always seek a deeper understanding of the unrealized potential in our situations and actions?

## PUTTING IT INTO PRACTICE: ONE EXAMPLE

Lara Lee, the president of Orchard Supply during a period when it was undergoing severe stress as an organization, recently spoke to a group of business leaders about bringing in this kind of waking-up practice to turn a business around. First of all, she pointed out, it is necessary to disrupt established patterns and habits. People have to notice whenever they are doing or thinking about things in a familiar way and choose to change or challenge how they are working. Next, she observed that it is important to form a premise about what is being missed or what might be a better approach and to use subsequent work to test it by including processes for employee self-examination and examination of the effects it produces when applied.

"Our team decided that we would, 'Always work from a living systems framework,'" Lee went on to say, sharing the mantra that she and her team adopted to help them stay conscious. Frameworks, she explained, bring coherence, discipline, and wholeness to a team's thinking, enabling it to avoid the habitual ruts that can stop a change process in its tracks. "Finally, and perhaps most importantly," Lee concluded, "we made a strong agreement to always reflect on the quality of our process, our thinking, and what they produced. This allowed us to test the integrity of our work, while setting the stage for improving it in the next round, especially when this involved moving into new arenas." This shift in approach was simple, challenging, fast-moving in the ripple effects it produced across and beyond the company, and transformational in the lives of many of its roughly six thousand employees.

What is so powerful and relevant about Lee's experience is that she was working with her team to help them transform their inner lives—the attitudes, beliefs, commitments, consciousness, and mental discipline that they could call on to transform their work and the company's. She was, in other words, helping them build their ability to think for themselves—to engage critically and systemically with any subject that they encountered. This shared strategy offered the overall guidance and direction they needed to make choices, but the change effort itself was based on inner capacity development. The creative energy it unleashed was awe-inspiring.

I hope it is apparent that the work Lee was doing with her company was not happening in little workshops or occasional leadership meetings. It was ubiquitous, an approach that informed everything they did. This is one of the reasons why it spread so quickly—sooner or later, nearly everyone in the company got to experience a different way of thinking and working and then began to incorporate these into their in-store meetings, planning sessions, and customer engagements. It worked because it was not piecemeal. The practices used were derived from the self-determination theory of knowing, and they were implemented everywhere at Orchard Supply.

## A Framework for Practice

In the preceding chapters, I have made the case for adopting the self-determination theory of knowledge, arguing that this is critical for preparing ourselves to respond with intelligence and nuance to the rapid, disruptive changes that we will experience in the twenty-first century. Next, I am going to introduce some of the practices that I have used to cultivate this theory and the disciplined thinking it is meant to foster. All were designed to grapple with the fact that, due to the domination of the external-authority theory of knowledge, most people have not learned to think for themselves and find the prospect of doing so unappealing. They resent it and have a strong tendency to resist it, possibly because they fear the loss of comfort that comes when they take full responsibility for themselves and the perceived loss of power when they give up their positions of expertise.

This puts those of us who choose to be change agents in a challenging position. We will necessarily need to discourage people from looking to us as the source of solutions. And we will need to encourage them to develop the capacity to discover new ways of working and learning. How do we do this in ways that take us out of the position of authority? We will need to develop in ourselves high levels of self-awareness and the ego strength to resist the mantle of authority, especially when it is being thrust onto us. We will also need to consistently apply a set of sophisticated practices that continually direct people's attention back to their own agency and development.

These practices are basically agnostic or neutral with regard to content, which is supplied by the circumstances in which they are applied. In my earlier books, I have offered many examples of how I have used the practices in particular situations. Those case studies are meant to illustrate practices in use, but they are definitely not intended to provide models or recipes to be copied. In this book, I have focused on the extraordinary experience I had working with Colgate South Africa, which demonstrates more fully than any other in my career what is possible when you trust individuals to be self-directing, encourage them to strengthen their capacities and increase their capabilities, and lead them to develop and innovate in response to a compelling community need.

The circumstances in South Africa were unique. In that historic moment, there was enormous pressure for radical change; workers from the townships knew that they could and must make a difference; and, at Colgate, we had in Stelios Tsezos a corporate leader who was willing to lay everything on the line to make it happen. We worked diligently for three and a half years to achieve an unprecedented transformation, and in the process, we grew a group of leaders who went on to take key roles in businesses, local communities, and the new South African government. Along the way, we evolved what we were doing, moment to moment, day by day. We had a general understanding of the practices we needed, but we created fresh applications in response to the specific conditions and people we were working with.

And this is what you must do with the practices I am offering here in this book. Apply the self-determining epistemology: think of the practices as riddles that can help you orient yourself to the work to be done, and then seek to discover your own approaches by surrendering yourself to the systems-actualization called for in the moment. Keep an eye out for any tendency to go on autopilot or copy what you or I or someone else has done in the past. These are almost always indicators that the external-authority theory of knowledge has snuck in again through the back door.

I have organized the four sets of six practices around the four terms of the Self-Determination Theory of Knowledge Tetrad: sourcing mind, systems intelligence, time binding, and long-thought processes. Each of the next four chapters is dedicated to one of these sets. For each set, I have developed a premise and distilled a principle that is intended to help readers hold in mind the whole of the point on the tetrad.

When taken together, the Self-Determination Theory of Knowledge Tetrad and the framework of twenty-four practices provides a powerful basis for initiating and sustaining the development of people who can manage their own thinking and state of being. The practices are also useful for designing events where people come together to move something forward in some way, with the aim of evolving their thinking as they do so. I am introducing them as a framework to reinforce the idea that this is a systemic whole, which cannot be adopted in a piecemeal fashion without undermining the philosophical integrity that allows it to be so powerful.

# Ninth Intermezzo

Fragmentation is perhaps the single most destructive result of the automatic, mechanistic approach to life. We see entities in isolation—a person, family, shop or school, lifeshed—as though they operated independently of the web of relationships that create their living context. To counter this strong cultural tendency and begin to see the world as a living whole requires a dedicated, ongoing exercise of will.

Nearly every institution in our lives works in a fragmenting way. Our education fragments the world into subjects, while the sciences atomize, dissect, and classify. We are at the mercy of our own fragmented and fragmenting mind, using it to break apart the outer world while oversimplifying our inner world. A key aspect of becoming self-determining is to exercise the will required to develop an authentic, conscious, and singular self that can dismantle this inner and outer fragmentation. We must learn to image whole systems at work, playing their roles within larger wholes.

## Capacity-Regenerating Questions: Will

- Pause to notice the ways that your education, training, career experience, or other influences are shaping the way you have been reading *No More Gold Stars*. What stood out as important to you and what in your past caused you to organize it into categories? Where did ideas seem recognizable and familiar because they aligned with things you have encountered before? In other words, can you observe yourself fragmenting or being fragmented? What is the outcome of this cherry-picking?

- Once you have brought this process into consciousness, ask yourself what is being lost. What are you missing from the whole that is trying to be conveyed? What is left behind in the whole of you when you read through the lens of a trained professional or expert?

- What would the implications be if you were to start every thinking process from a whole at work? Do you know how or where you might begin? If you were to do this, how might you have a different experience of the world, your work, the place you live, the people you know? What changes in you when you approach the world in this way?

# Chapter Ten

# Sourcing Mind Practices

In chapter 4, I stated that in a tetrad framework, *ground* refers to a starting place with the highest conceivable potential given one's current best understanding of the situation under consideration and the way the world works. Here I will provide a set of practices that I have used for developing and working from *sourcing mind*, the ground point on the Self-Determination Theory of Knowledge Tetrad (Figure 4).

**Figure 4: Self-Determination Theory of Knowledge Tetrad:**
**Sourcing Mind at the Ground Point.**

## Sourcing Mind

My premise with regard to sourcing mind is that *it is necessary to activate an internal process that allows me to track my own thinking and its evolution; otherwise, I remain trapped in my conditioning, limited to the external-authority worldview.* *Sourcing* is the key word here. Our minds are filled with ideas and beliefs that we have brought in from outside ourselves, often without any awareness. We usually do not know the sources of our thoughts, prejudices, and firmly held convictions. This is exacerbated by our cultural conditioning, which prompts us to seek outside expertise or opinions as the basis for developing our own thoughts.

A sourcing mind requires us to begin with a refusal: *I refuse to accept that any thought or opinion, neither my own nor anyone else's, is whole and complete.* A sourcing mind challenges the conditioning on which its thinking is based in order to see things anew. This assumes that any person's ability to develop understanding can and should evolve. It is always possible to take understanding deeper and to make it more specific, and the discipline of doing so is key to developing ourselves and our species.

To place conscious attention on *how* we develop understanding, we must also create an appropriate restraint on our tendency to jump to inadequately examined conclusions: *I must disrupt my mechanicalness.* This requires a discipline or method for interrupting automatic patterns of response. In other words, we must add a second layer of conscious practice and observe both how we are processing the thoughts of those who might influence us and how we are sourcing our own: What paradigm is framing this thought, and what worldview informs it? What framework would expand what is under consideration? What state of being am I in, and how might it give rise to this thought or way of thinking? For example, am I reacting to an idea or situation, and is this an appropriate state of being for the task at hand?

Questions like these enable us to overcome autopilot and engage in disciplined, ongoing examination of our mental processing. This is the reliable *ground* provided by sourcing mind.

## Six Practices for Developing Sourcing Mind

With regard to the practice of developing sourcing mind, I have distilled my premise into a principle that is intended to remind us what we are aiming for. There is a popular bumper sticker slogan that captures the spirit I have in mind: *Don't believe everything you think!* To put this in more positive terms: *Examine your beliefs—always remember to look for the sources of your beliefs and the thoughts, choices, and actions that flow from them, especially when these beliefs appear to be self-evident.*

I.  ***Introduce conscious shock.*** Because there is a strong tendency for people to stay within well-established, habitual patterns of thought and action, it can be very difficult to get them to adopt a genuinely fresh view. Even when one introduces or proposes profoundly new ways of thinking about something, people will fit these new ideas into preexisting contexts and assumptions. For this reason, it is necessary to introduce a shock, to snap people out of their routines and upgrade the quality of energy and potential informing their mental processes so that they become increasingly conscious. Sometimes this can take the form of pointing out the difference between what people say they are doing and what they are actually doing. Other times, it can mean invoking an entirely different order of possibility than the one people are currently working on.

   Whatever delivers the shock, its purpose is to lift people out of their current existence, breaking their attachments to and identification with the way things are. This enables them to refocus their attention on the deeper potential that could be manifested from their work, enabling them to sense something new and meaningful flowing into their world and to know that they can find within themselves ways to be part of it.

   *Colgate South Africa*: Although we used the practice of conscious shock periodically to upgrade our work at Colgate, the most important shock was introduced at the very beginning. Stelios Tsezos first addressed employees, and then we called together employees with people from local government and key local businesses. What Tsezos said to us all set the ground for everything afterward. Referring to the constitutional mandate that within five years management in South African companies must reflect the racial and cultural diversity of the country, he laid down a visionary challenge. "What if," he asked, "instead of taking sixty months to make this change, we do it in six?" The effect was electrifying, terrifying, and inspiring. In that moment, we all knew that we needed to do what he was proposing, that it represented a future worth striving for. And, in fact, we pulled it off.

2. **Examine premises.** A conscious shock can open a doorway, a willingness to change. But it needs to be followed up with an ongoing, disciplined practice, whereby people learn to examine their foundational beliefs about reality as it is and as it should be. In most of us, these beliefs are culturally biased and were instilled when we were very young. Although they may be invisible to us, they can be powerful impediments to the change we wish to create. Learning to examine our beliefs—tracing them back to their sources and forward to their effects on our behaviors, choices, and actions—is both urgently necessary and mentally liberating. Once a group learns to do this work, it finds that many of the things that appeared to block forward motion begin to melt away.

   *Colgate South Africa*: The conscious shock that Tsezos introduced raised an immediate and seemingly insoluble problem. The apartheid system had prohibited most of South Africa's Black population from gaining any kind of formal education or professional training. How were we going to promote Black people to top levels of management when they were simply unqualified and when it would take years to build their qualifications?

   The unexamined belief behind this question was that formal education is a better preparation for business management than lived experience. We demonstrated the opposite. Uneducated township workers were consistently more systemic and creative in their thinking than trained professionals, and when given the freedom to direct themselves, they turned the company's financial performance around with breathtaking speed.

3. **Question authority.** One of the consistent sources of failure within existing machine models of social and business systems is that they derive insight from narrow (or even theoretical) examples and apply them generally. Referred to as "best practices," this approach is generic, abstract, life denying, and therefore spirit killing. As my own experience demonstrates, local intelligence based on real experience within specific contexts offers a far more powerful basis for radical innovation than any number of pricey

consultants. But this intelligence needs to be unlocked and developed—freed from the debilitating belief that we need an outside expert to find us an answer or that someone else has already come up with the best answer, and thus we do not need to make the effort ourselves.

*Colgate South Africa:* We were able to supplant this tendency to rely on best practices and generic expert opinion by building people's ability to think concretely about how they engaged in their day-to-day work. We held regular workshops in which we asked people to use frameworks to examine their lived experience and apply their insights to the work they were doing. This became a ground for understanding what was truly going on in the situations they were trying to affect and enabled them to create guidelines and principles that specifically addressed the needs of real people in real contexts.

Because we were doing this in actual work teams, which were applying their insights to actual work, we promoted a direct relationship between those who generated concepts and the work these concepts would inform. As a result, all workers were involved in testing and upgrading their ideas based on effectiveness, using frameworks they had practiced with during workshop sessions. Outside experts or evaluators were rarely required, and when they were, it was almost always only to address specific technical issues.

4. ***Embrace Socratic questioning.*** The antidote to practices that derive from the external-authority theory of knowledge is already present in Western culture, with roots that go back thousands of years. It was vividly demonstrated through the life and teachings of the ancient Greek philosopher Socrates, who was committed to growing the capacity of his students—and all other Athenian citizens—to look within themselves as the way to understand the world. "The unexamined life is not worth living," he famously said, and the ideas and passions his students experienced in the present moment offered the perfect opportunity for developing this capacity. They learned to question the sources and effects of their thinking and thereby to think for themselves. Socrates was particularly conscious of the hazards of arrogance and hubris, and their relationship to certitude. He emphasized the importance of humility, embracing consciousness of how we know as a prerequisite to learning.

*Colgate South Africa*: We understood that we needed to grow a developmental infrastructure within Colgate South Africa if the creativity, commitment to growth, and heightened sense of spirit and will were to be sustained. Conscious shock is like fireworks; it wakes people up and excites and inspires them, but the effect will last only a little while unless it is supported by an ongoing developmental process. To accomplish this, we created the role of resource—people who help others reconnect to the sources of things—and began building people's ability to engage in Socratic questioning in order to take on this role.

Resources were part of every workshop, planning session, and group decision-making process. Their role was to introduce frameworks and guide groups with probing questions, helping them to evolve the quality of their thinking by grounding it in concrete experience. In short order, people throughout the company were practicing sophisticated systems thinking at all times. No wonder they were able to so quickly respond to rapidly changing social, economic, and political dynamics.

5. ***Disrupt certainty.*** A subtle relationship grows over time between ourselves and the beliefs we are certain about. We come to identify ourselves with our certainties so strongly that to challenge them is to challenge our identities and, with them, our self-worth. This can become an intellectual and emotional trap, and it is the reason I recommend that Socratic questioning be practiced in the way that Socrates demonstrated: live and in dialogue, in the presence of people who are witnessing and applying what they are hearing to their own situations.

I call this activity *the fishbowl* and find that it is very effective for helping people dislodge rigid and unexamined beliefs. One person agrees to have their thinking challenged by a resource working with an agreed-upon subject and systemic framework. Meanwhile, a group of silent witnesses engage in self-examination, using the same framework and the same kind of questioning, as though they were themselves in the fishbowl.

Then, based on what has been revealed through dialogue, the person in the fishbowl uses a second framework to reflect on the experience as a way to consciously anchor it in themself. This reflection not only helps them and the other participants elevate their thinking, it also develops important inner qualities such as agility, flexibility, imperturbability, and the ability to manage reactivity and ego attachments.

The experience also serves the resource, who, if they are to serve the inner development of others, must develop impeccability of attention, humility, caring, and flexibility of thought through the practice of self-questioning.

*Colgate South Africa:* A few months into the work at Colgate, we were in a meeting of three hundred people when I first asked if someone would volunteer to be in the fishbowl. One man stood up and told us that in his tribe, the ancient traditions had been translated into the apartheid era by recognizing that boys leaving home to work, often in dangerous jobs, were undergoing a rite of passage. As a critical part of this ritual, the boys were taken under the wing of uncles or elders, who would challenge them to reflect on what they were learning from this life-changing step.

For this man, the relationship had been broken prematurely when his uncle died, and he felt that he had never completed his initiation into adulthood. He saw the fishbowl as an opportunity to complete the process. I asked him, "What is the question that you would like to work on?"

"What is my life for?" he responded.

It was such a powerful moment that I can still feel it.

I asked him a series of exploratory questions based on a familiar framework that we had been working with across the company. My questions invited him to look at the differences among a life lived reactively, a life lived from ego, and a life lived in service to some purpose. Before long, he and half the room had tears streaming down their faces.

When we ended the fishbowl, the room erupted into song and dance, which was the way all local tribal peoples celebrated important moments. Then they sat down again and settled into a deep silence as each reflected on what was being called for from them—regenerating both the work they were doing together at Colgate and their tribal traditions in service to the transformation of themselves, their nation, and the world.

6. *Use self-assessment.* Assessment is a natural and necessary aspect of learning and development. However, due to the collective bias toward seeking outside authority and validation, our ability to accurately assess

ourselves has largely atrophied. For example, think about how we train our children. "Good job!" we tell them, trying to be encouraging and directive. It rarely occurs to us to ask them to tell us what they were trying to accomplish, how they think they did, and what they would like to improve next time.

When the self-assessment muscle does not develop, a dependency on outside authority takes hold and gets amplified, year after year. Most adults report that they cannot improve without other people's feedback. Everyone loses when this happens. Those who are assessed by others lose faith in their own ability to see themselves accurately, to manage themselves, and to take on challenges beyond their current capability. Those who give the feedback never learn to resource the people around them, relying instead on the degenerative habit of telling them what to think. This pattern is corrosive to teams and organizations, which lose their agency and self-accountability because they never build the capacity or culture that supports independent thought and accurate self-evaluation.

*Colgate South Africa*: Right from the beginning, we set out to break this destructive pattern, particularly because it was a symbolic reminder of colonialism and apartheid, during which time a small White minority had told everyone else what to do and how to do it. We laid out several managing principles that were shared across the company, principles that were designed to enable everyone to self-manage with regard to what we were collectively aiming to create.

As workers rotated through various leadership roles, we made it explicit that they were not to share their opinions or judgments about those they worked with but were, instead, to focus on building capability. We articulated this managing principle as "Your job is to assess yourself with regard to your ableness to give people the capability to assess themselves." Workers named this practice "mirroring" because they were expecting the same thing from themselves that they hoped to see in others.

We made a ritual of asking rotating leaders to begin each meeting with an assessment of how well they were building self-assessment capacity in the company. Before long, the idea put down deep roots in their thinking and approach. The ability to self-assess was built quickly, because the demands of survival meant that most tribal people were still pretty good at being self-directed. They just needed an environment and culture within which to exercise and develop this innate capability.

# Tenth Intermezzo

Chapter 10 worked from *sourcing mind*, the ground point of the Self-Determination Theory of Knowledge Tetrad. In the following set of questions, I invite you to reflect on sourcing mind as the ground for your reading process.

## Capacity-Regenerating Questions

- What are your go-to sources for conducting your thinking? How much are they in your head as you read? What role do they play in your conscious or unconscious evaluation of whether the text is consistent with your current values and beliefs?

- What new ways to question these sources have you discovered, either from *No More Gold Stars* or from the conscious reflection you have brought to your reading?

- Based on your own observations, how important is it to examine your way of perceiving and interpreting, both during and after reading?

# CHAPTER ELEVEN

# SYSTEMS INTELLIGENCE PRACTICES

We turn now to the goal point on the Self-Determination Theory of Knowledge Tetrad (Figure 5). In chapter 4, I stated that in any tetrad framework, *goal* refers to the transformation in a system's state that enables it to pursue new orders or natures of work and effect. In this case, our goal is the development of *systems intelligence*.

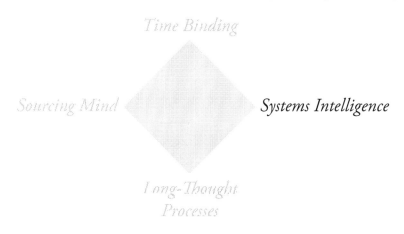

**Figure 5: Self-Determination Theory of Knowledge Tetrad: Systems Intelligence at the Goal Point.**

## Systems Intelligence

My premise with regard to systems intelligence is that *if we understand that all living systems are intelligent—and if we have the humility and willingness to develop our own intelligence—then in our dialogues with them, they will enable us to discover the roles that we need to play in their evolution.* I have repeatedly said that learning to think for ourselves, becoming self-determining and self-directed, is key to learning to live on and contribute to Earth. With this in mind, I think of a goal as working at three interconnected levels to produce *results*, which ripple out to manifest *outcomes*, and therefore eventually to generate *effects*.

At the level of results, the self-determination theory of knowledge produces people who think for themselves and therefore repeatedly and reliably produce new thoughts and understandings rather than simply recycle old, unexamined ones. At the level of outcomes, independent thinking further manifests as the mental freedom, capacity, and agility needed to play contributing roles within dynamically evolving living systems. At the level of effects, it emerges as the intellectual or spiritual maturity required to fully reintegrate human beings as conscious participants in the work of planetary evolution.

My premise also speaks of the humility we need to image ourselves as the children of forests, grasslands, and estuaries, rather than conceive of ourselves as their dominating governors. Our humble goal should be to gratefully embrace and take responsibility for the distinctive gift of human intelligence by doing the hard work to develop it in service to life's purposes.

## Six Practices for Developing Systems Intelligence

My principle for keeping the goal of systems intelligence in mind is *think systems!— cultivate the discipline to manage mental processes toward living systems consciousness and away from the pernicious influence of linear, mechanistic thinking.*

I.   **Use systemic frameworks with consciousness.** Mechanistic thinking and adopting the thinking of others without conscious critique are hard habits to break. Whenever we encounter something that has a clear form or structure, we have a strong tendency to accept it without question. This may be because its currency or its existence alone suggests that it has something going for it. Physical structures (such as city streets and highways), processes (such as accepted ways to organize tasks), and beliefs (such as conviction that hierarchies are the best way to organize people ) demand conscious, focused observation and analysis if we are to successfully question them. Our continual task is to unearth the underlying assumptions that inform the ways our minds are shaping reality.

Enabling this effort as part of daily life is the purpose of living systems frameworks. When used correctly, they empower us to embody systems intelligence as we engage in life, offering a basis for growing increasingly coherent and deep understanding of previously unexplored phenomena. This is a key to developing independent thinking, but frameworks only work when we use them to manage thinking in the very moment when it is occurring. As an added benefit, with dedicated practice over time we can learn to use systemic frameworks to gain insight into increasingly higher orders of complexity, which is necessary if we wish to work regeneratively within larger living systems (such as our lifesheds and the complex weaving of them together that makes up the living Earth).

*Colgate South Africa*: Early in our work, we established a large and diverse *core team*. Their role was to develop an essence understanding of the company and the context it was operating in and to set the direction that would enable the company to become a transformational force. The core team developed a set of seven managing principles that would guide the company as it undertook the implementation of a *noncompetitive contribution hierarchy*. These principles were circulated among the market field teams (which comprised every member of the organization) for reflection and upgrades.

One of these field teams came back with a clear response: "What's missing is an eighth principle that speaks to the need to sustain consciousness. We propose, '*To remain conscious, always begin, continue, and end with a framework.*' "

Needless to say, the core team was delighted. "How did we miss this?" they wondered. "It's so obviously critical." They sent the new principle to all the other market teams, who also wondered how they had missed it. In short order, it was adopted across the company.

2. ***Make it concrete and specific—one of one.*** In his popular book *The End of Average: Unlocking Our Potential by Embracing What Makes Us Different*, Harvard University researcher Todd Rose points out that there is a dark side to generalizing. In the process, we lose contact with the particular, and this has deeply destructive consequences for how we relate to one another and the world.[11] For example, it is critical to engage with children as singular persons, not as exemplars of certain phases of development. The latter represents the life-denying intellectual laziness that is all too common in our world, substituting a generic or abstract idea for the actual living phenomenon that is standing before us.

A vast majority of us are interested in *demographics* rather than the *demos* themselves. We categorize, typologize, and shoehorn people into boxes that will never actually fit them, on the assumption that a little bit of generic knowledge is all that we need to locate them correctly in their respective social machines. Humans are not machines; they are individuals, one of one, as are their organizations, communities, cultures, and bioregions. Respecting them as such requires us to relearn how to do something that was obvious to our ancestors: adopt as a basic orientation to the world that *each living being is unique, numinous, and ultimately uncategorizable*. I believe that this adamant refusal to genericize the world is the key to reversing the pervasive denial of aliveness that informs almost everything we do.

*Colgate South Africa:* As it turned out, making things concrete and specific was central to the way we worked in South Africa, in part because the working teams demanded it. I remember a session where one worker was making a presentation about progress on his promise beyond ableness. About twenty minutes in, another worker raised his hand and asked, "Sorry, but who are we talking about here? I can't get a picture in my mind of the whole, living being."

All around him, people nodded and laughed. They realized that they had been following along with the presentation, using generic ideas and stereotypes to make sense of it. Not one of them had a specific being in mind. "We need to adopt this as a rule! Our only rule," said another worker. "Never work on anything without having in mind the specific being that the work

11  Todd Rose, *The End of Average: Unlocking Our Potential by Embracing What Makes Us Different* (New York: HarperCollins, 2017).

is intended to serve." Otherwise, they knew, they would lose connection to concrete reality, which was the source not only of their creativity but also of their sense that what they were doing was meaningful and important.

The workers loved telling this story, telling on themselves about the time that the entire room had been lulled into complacency, as a way to get everyone else in the company to understand the importance of adopting their single rule.

3. ***Work indirectly and qualitatively.*** My understanding of transformational change is informed by the discoveries of modern physics, including that the universe is whole and entangled. This implies that working directly on any one thing will always elicit a systemic response (such as pushback). This is the source of unintended consequences, that *any direct action* will yield a host of unpredictable reactions across multiple nested systems. A second implication is that working indirectly and qualitatively within a whole system results in the system's increased capacity to transform itself.

Translated to the human arena, this means that the psychological and social complexity of human beings demands indirect qualitative work. This view stands in opposition to that of the behaviorists, who denied the relevance of internal human processes and therefore denied the relevance of any qualitative differences among them. In a nutshell, for behaviorists, human life could be reduced to behaviors, and behaviors could be shaped by direct interventions in the form of rewards and punishments. From my perspective, this approach completely ignores the potential in humans for creativity, self-management, will, steadfastness, caring, profundity, and uncountable other valuable qualities. Indirect work seeks to grow these qualities by cultivating the conditions that enable them to emerge, such as consciousness, capability, and a developmental culture. Behaviorism's external-authority theory of knowledge seeks to manage behavior within narrowly defined limits, while the self-direction theory of knowledge seeks to tear the roof off human possibility.

*Colgate South Africa*: In practical terms, indirect work became the province of the company's *resources*, those workers who took on responsibility for growing capability across the company. Almost from day one, we eliminated the role of supervisors and managers, helping the people who had played those roles transition into the role of resource. Of course, building capability is something that any responsible company attempts to do with its people, but companies almost always use an external authority approach. The supervisor, who is presumably better qualified than their supervisees, figures out how to do something and then trains their teams to embed the needed capability.

A resource, on the other hand, challenges people to develop their own thinking about what is needed and how to accomplish it. A rapidly transforming organization will naturally call for many natures of capability, and different resources tend to be drawn toward one or another of these as their own promise beyond ableness. Some find themselves helping to build technical capabilities while others focus on activities that require increasing ability to manage complexity, such as product conceptualization, marketing, or strategic thinking.

In support of the strong culture of self-management and self-accountability that we built at Colgate South Africa, nearly all resources were called on to help their colleagues build the capability to manage their state of being from moment to moment; in this case, to become more and more imperturbable in the face of chaos, stress, or even violence. This had the ancillary effect of growing their critical leadership capacity in service to their townships.

4. ***Trust lived experience.*** All the practices to source systems intelligence assume that we can trust our lived experience, providing we subject this experience to deep examination and reflection. If we do not learn to trust our experience, then we have no way to counteract or supplant the authoritarian and mechanistic worldview influences that bombard us. Yet this trust is under constant assault by systems that have been designed to condition and control our behaviors and sense of autonomy.

This is why, from a young age, I fought for my contrarian perspective so that I would have some way of restraining the impulse to go along in order to get along—and so that I could have more of the kind of stimulation that woke me up to the whole beautiful world. When colonizers subjugate an Indigenous people, the first thing they set out to do is to undermine self-determination by rooting out mental autonomy. They make the assault in many arenas, but usually, they start with education. In my experience, Indigenous educational practices focus on the development of capability to ask and explore questions by oneself. Only when a person has developed their own answers—or theories—is it appropriate for them to approach an elder and ask for their perspective.

Modern Western education focuses on the opposite: the system supplies the answer, and the learner's job is to memorize it. Over time, we learn not only to distrust our own experience and ability to think things through, but to not even consider it, and this creates in us the mentality of abject dependency. This is precisely the aim of behaviorism—to weaken trust in ourselves so that we can be more easily colonized and controlled.

*Colgate South Africa*: Walking into my role at Colgate, I was conscious of the temptation to provide answers for people (and to really like the answers I came up with!), so I laid out some ground rules for myself: no one-on-one sessions and no Q&A. I was dealing with an interesting cultural context in that these were people for whom *everything* in their work lives had come as directives from above. At the same time, they had been forced in their private lives to be highly self-reliant.

We brought this contradiction to a boil in one of the first sessions I led. I had given breakout groups an exercise, and when they came back, one of the groups volunteered to share what they had done. A young man stood up and began reporting back to me on what I had said and how they were going to implement it. Like a stern teacher, I cut him off immediately.

"Let's get clear right from the start," I told him. "No reporting back on what I said or think. You are to do your own thinking, and if it's really yours, then it's going to disagree with mine at least some of the time. And don't ask me what I think of your ideas because I'm not going to tell you! It's not my job to supply approval; it's your job."

The poor fellow rocked back on his heels from my intensity, but I felt I *had* to cut him off because it was desperately important to break the pattern of dependency on me as an authority figure. It was hard for me to over-come my politeness in a situation where I was meeting people for the first time, but I was terrified that if I did not, then we would never accomplish the critical transformation in agency and self-accountability that would be required. I needn't have worried about him, though, because he and the rest of the group got the idea instantly and went back to do the real work I assigned them, laughing and shaking their heads in amazement. When they came back, they did that wonderful thing that was so characteristic of the place and people: they burst into song, embodying the cultural wisdom and tribal histories that brought meaning to the questions and challenges we were facing together.

5. ***Image life at work.*** The human mind has the capacity to produce complex, vivid images. This is useful when it comes to developing systems intelligence. Unfortunately, we have mostly been encouraged to place this capacity in service to imagination—to make things up in our minds, a process that almost always builds off of some fragmentary idea, wish, or worry. However, there is another, far more powerful use for this image-making function, which I call *imaging*. In contrast to imagination, imaging is a disciplined anchoring of attention to the reality of an entity, endeavoring to experience it as alive, whole, and interacting with its larger systemic context. Imaging enables us to perceive characteristics of a situation that are otherwise unavailable to us, such as wholeness, entanglement, role, dynamism, evolutionary tendencies, core qualities, and the generation and exchange of value.

Of course, it helps to be searching for these, which is why frameworks are so useful for directing our thinking about living systems. It is also import-ant to sincerely want to understand what we are trying to image, and this requires us to restrain the tendency to project our egos, assumptions, and foregone conclusions. It also requires us to overcome the bias toward frag-mentation that we have learned from the scientific method, which teaches us to focus on a single aspect of a system while isolating all other variables. Imaging is the opposite of this, an attempt to see all the system dynamics at work and interacting within a value-adding process. In this way it offers a basis for a non-fragmenting science.

We are the only ones who can keep ourselves honest in this regard. It is up to each of us to observe and examine the quality of our imaging and the integrity of the insights and conclusions we draw from it. When we do so, we develop a distinctly human way of accessing the livingness of things, something that could be encouraged in children but is generally neglected in their education.

*Colgate South Africa:* The tribal people I worked with in South Africa were good at imaging from the start, but it was nevertheless important for them to develop ableness to clearly distinguish imaging from imagination. We practiced the difference. We would talk about or act out a particular subject from a human perspective, as though we were in charge. Workers compared this to being playwrights, able to identify the problems and dictate the solutions in their imaginary drama. Then I would ask them to experience the same subject from the perspective of the system that it was embedded in, forgetting about their own opinions and interpretations and instead listening to the ways that the system expressed its life. They called this spirit-writing because they were taking instruction from the spirit of what they wished to understand. From this place, they could readily enact or dance or sing the inner story of the system as a living, working being, and this radically shifted the way they engaged with it.

6. ***Remember the role of humans.*** It distresses me when I hear otherwise rational and well-meaning people say that the problem on the planet is humans and that all other living systems on Earth would be better off without our species. On the one hand, this idea is hopeless, despairing, even nihilistic. On the other, it expresses blindness to the potential contribution that human consciousness could make to evolution. This blindness prevents us from doing the hard work of consciousness development that living systems expect and require of us. From my perspective, despair is a form of laziness, an avoidance of responsibility that demonstrates the immaturity that human beings need to grow out of if we are to play our role in the biosphere. The problem is that some human societies have constructed systems that prevent their members from growing up, and, as a result, they have more or less forgotten that this is a possibility.

Remember, in the twentieth century, we collectively adopted methods of education and conditioning to make people machinelike. This was in response to the rapid evolution of industrial systems that required people to integrate themselves into vastly larger machines—school systems, factories, industries. Because, under the right material circumstances and with coercive means, it is possible to ingrain in workers habits of mental torpor.

This effort was highly successful. It set aside concerns about the souls, wills, and creative dispositions of individuals, the genius that is unique to each of us, in favor of mass-produced and readily manageable behaviors within entire populations. When treating people as commodities, it is neither useful nor relevant to encourage them to think for themselves or to take responsibility for what their thinking produces. Once the behaviors and skills have been successfully put in place, the worker is ready, finished—at least until the next set of behaviors and skills are needed.

By contrast, conscious participation in the evolution of Earth is our potential, our gift, and our destiny. Consciousness takes work. You could say that it both grows from and focuses the other practices described here. When we are born, consciousness exists as a latent possibility within us. But unless it is developed, we do not access its power to build will and purposefulness in our lives, defaulting instead to mental processes that emphasize reactivity, conditioned automatism, or sensitivity.

Unfortunately, there are very few schools or educational philosophies that place consciousness at the center of their work, a deficit that badly needs to be addressed because harmonization with Earth's planetary systems is a critical human concern. Consciousness's value to evolution comes from the way it allows us to perceive and cultivate the living potential in systems, rather than be trapped by existence and entropy. Remembering that humans' role is to supply conscious energy to living processes is a core aspect of the self-determination theory of knowledge. It provides a necessary source of motivation because it reminds us of why this work, which is so demanding, is also so important.

*Colgate South Africa*: Workers' promises beyond ableness were developed out of their inquiry into the role that they and the company might play in the evolution of the country. As part of their proposal, we asked each person to develop an introduction that described some gap between the potential they saw for their community and the current conditions that existed there. Then we asked them to speak to how they could develop their consciousness with regard to this potential and what role they and the company might play in developing public consciousness about it. This was a critical dimension of the thinking that workers brought to the projects and initiatives they undertook because it recognized a need for indirect work. It was not enough to just do things for your township, no matter how well-intentioned. For real change to occur, you needed to do them in a way that engaged the will and consciousness of others.

In one of my favorite examples, a worker was spending quite a bit of time with women entrepreneurs who were trying to create small local businesses in Soweto, where he lived. As he watched the women struggle with the competing demands of raising their children and creating a livelihood, he had the insight that children's oral health was a major issue affecting their families' well-being. Dealing with dental problems after they occurred was disruptive and costly for impoverished parents, but traditional methods of prevention had been lost, and modern products, such as tubes of toothpaste, were financially beyond reach. The worker began to see an opportunity to connect local entrepreneurship with oral health through a project that enabled women to create businesses delivering small, affordable amounts of toothpaste to township families on a regular basis.

By shining a light on the systemic importance of oral health to children and families, the worker was able to grow social consciousness and a cultural commitment to instilling good toothcare practices, enrolling a whole system of stakeholders to support the process. At the same time, he was helping Colgate make its oral care products available to a population that had previously had no access to them. It was innovations like these that enabled Colgate not only to evolve the quality of life that was available in the townships, but also to do so in ways that enabled the company to grow.

# Eleventh Intermezzo

As we move to *systems intelligence*, the goal in our tetrad, it is important to maintain connection with sourcing mind. The dynamic relationships among the terms are what makes this a living systems framework. Because in this context self-direction is oriented toward actualizing systems, it makes sense that the sourcing mind is moving us to sources that will allow us to gain systems intelligence. With the following set of questions, I invite you to reflect on this as a goal for your reading process.

## Capacity-Regenerating Questions

- What are your favorite causes or issues? How are they influencing the way that you are reading? From what stage of development are you connecting to these causes (for example, personal investment or personal improvement versus systems-actualization)?

- What underlies these causes? What new ways to investigate and understand them have you discovered, either from your reading or from the conscious reflection you have brought to your reading? Have you gained systems intelligence regarding them? To what extent do they affect your energy? What do they open your mind to?

- Based on your observations, how important is it to examine the causes that motivate you, the sources that fuel them, and the level from which you are engaging them?

# Chapter Twelve

# Time-Binding Practices

In a tetrad framework, *direction* refers to the way one brings spirit into efforts to provide guidance and a sense of aspiration, lifting oneself beyond the constraints of existence. In this chapter, I will offer a set of six practices I have used for orienting to *time binding*, the direction point on the Self-Determination Theory of Knowledge Tetrad (Figure 6).

*Time Binding*

Sourcing Mind

Systems Intelligence

Long-Thought Processes

**Figure 6: Self-Determination Theory of Knowledge Tetrad:
Time Binding at the Direction Point.**

Time binding, with its emphasis on the evolution of human consciousness and wisdom, supplies the impulse and guidance that helps us continually regenerate the will and spirit needed for self-determination. My premise with regard to time binding is that *human consciousness has the potential to make unique contributions to evolution when it enables each subsequent generation to deepen its capacity for understanding the underlying imperatives and processes of social and planetary systems.*

As I discussed in chapter 3, Alfred Korzybski distinguished among the roles of plants, which he described as *energy binding*, animals, which he described as *space binding*, and humans, which he described as *time binding*. Of course, we humans also function as energy and space binders, a reflection of our evolutionary history. We preserve the capacity to digest, distribute, and metabolize nutrients, and we very much shape our habitats. Indeed, these perfectly natural aspects of human activity, when unconsciously amplified by human intelligence, give rise to many of our destructive effects in the world. Time binding, on the other hand, is the means by which we grow the wisdom necessary for beneficial contributions to living systems. It is the attribute of intelligence that allows us to harness the experience of the past in order to project ourselves into an imageable future. And, so far as we know, on Earth it is unique to human intelligence.

Given our potential for time binding, shouldn't each human generation be progressively better at caring for one another and the planet? That we so clearly are not indicates how few of us are devoting ourselves to this critical activity and what an enormous amount of human potential remains untapped. With regard to development of this human potential, there is no endpoint, no moment when we arrive at the perfect, final, and therefore static truth about the cosmos. The evolution of living systems is dynamic and ongoing, and thus, so is the evolution of our understanding of life.

Unlimited opportunity exists for us humans to use time binding as a way to stay current with evolution, rather than perpetually lag behind. Time binding implies both a bottom and a top line. Bottom line, we humans must wise up. A lot more of us must actively engage in developing understanding and resourcing development of this capacity in others. Top line, there is no ceiling to the potential for human wisdom—we will never run out of questions that can take us further.

## Six Time-Binding Practices

Here is the principle distilled from my premise, intended to keep us oriented as we put time binding into practice: *contribute consciousness to evolution—develop the unique capacity of human consciousness to discern the arc of evolution through time in order to evolve the contributions we make to evolutionary processes.*

1. ***Never do anything the same way twice.*** An article of faith in the present era is that methods must be scalable to be viable. This means translating every creative insight or design into a template, formula, best practice, or model for mass production—the apotheosis of machine thinking and its drive to genericize the world. I cringe every time someone says to me, "Well, this is great, but can we scale it?" They are essentially asking how to eliminate the need to engage intelligently and creatively with living beings, self-to-self, in each present moment. Over the last century, machine thinking has reconceptualized farms and schools as factories, retail stores as consumer interfaces in global distribution chains, living ecosystems as repositories of natural resources, and human minds as biological computers. It is a very effective way to take the livingness out of living things, which makes it ironic—and counterproductive—that this is the approach most often used to address the multiple, ramifying crises of life on our planet.

   I have a simple but powerful antidote: insist on starting fresh in every encounter. As my colleague Charlie Krone used to say, "Everything for someone, nothing for the shelf." Do not use preexisting ideas or methods; that puts us right back into the trap of the authoritative expert. Insist instead on exercising the discipline to invent new ideas and methods out of the raw materials presented by the context—the people, places, and processes that will be affected in present time by any actions that are taken. In this way, understanding and capability will evolve with every new task, along with the outcomes and effects that can be generated.

   I know that this violates conventional organizational thinking about what is practical and possible—that is exactly my point. I know from direct experience that this approach is not only practical and possible, but that it will generate extraordinary improvements in performance. But this is so if and only if one cultivates, in oneself and those one works with, practices based on the self-determination theory of knowledge. Otherwise, the only choice is to borrow and copy, either from higher levels in the chain of command, one's own past thinking, or so-called experts.

*Colgate South Africa*: We created something that the teams came to call a *stop exercise*. Every time a group needed to design a presentation, a meeting, or even a new product offering, they would first stop themselves and ask, "How do we make this relevant, timely, and precise?" This would launch them into an inquiry about who they were designing for, what value they were seeking to create, and where they were in their process at *this* moment. In a short time, this broke the strong tendency to recycle old ideas and led to new patterns in how people were working together.

Instead of saying, as teams so often do, "We already thought about this two weeks ago. Does anybody have notes on what we said?" they would ask themselves, "How has the situation evolved since we last thought about this, and therefore how do *we* need to evolve?" Instead of creating a prefabricated presentation or customizing a generic one (like those dreaded PowerPoints that we all hate to sit through), they would shape their material specifically to the person or persons who were going to be in the room and make it relevant to them in the moment. The stop exercise put in place a form of taboo that rapidly shifted the culture of the company. People quickly learned to regenerate their thinking for every situation so that they were always seeing it anew, or else they could expect to be challenged by their peers.

2. ***Actualize and potentialize simultaneously.*** One bizarre outcome of the way we currently organize our societies is that work, which focuses on creating some kind of value for someone, is completely divorced from education, which focuses on acquiring knowledge and skills. This is true even though students learn more effectively and with greater enjoyment when what they are studying can be immediately applied to something meaningful. On the other side, workers are much more inspired by work when they can see that they are making a difference in the world and that they are growing their capabilities in the process. Even large, sophisticated companies put their workforces through batch or programmatic training programs, which are conducted by experts independently of participants'

daily work and designed to instill generic skills that may or may not end up being relevant.

This is nonsensical! When we invite people to think about their work and what it intends to serve, while demanding that they never think about it in the same way twice, we create unlimited opportunities for learning and development *right in the flow of work itself.* We are asking people to actualize—to bring an idea into material existence, to discover and build more potential into it and, as a result, into themselves as well. With a value-adding view of the world, we are always seeking to evolve the value of our efforts. Education and contribution become completely integral and synergistic with regard to one another, and this radically increases the speed and ubiquity of innovation.

*Colgate South Africa*: We particularly emphasized this practice whenever a team took on new projects, and it became part of project leaders' promises beyond ableness. They would gather their teams to design what they called *parallel processing.* Because these workers loved expressing things kinesthetically, they would often act out their answers to a set of questions designed to elicit creativity around three parallel aspects of the task they were taking on: how they needed to function, who they could become in the process, and their intended outcomes.

They started with a stop exercise, asking themselves, "If we were doing this project the old way, the colonial way, what would it look like?" This gave them a baseline to remind them of what they did not want to do so that they could catch themselves in the act whenever they fell into old habits. Then they would ask, "What framework do we want to use to lift this project up to a new level? How do we improve our understanding and our ability to work together as we get this done? What is a deeper source of motivation that will help us stay on track when we run into difficulties?" Because each project team created their own approaches to answering these questions, they were then able to evaluate (and celebrate) what they accomplished at all these levels.

3.  ***Work within a living oral tradition.*** As a young child, I used to love spending time with my Mohawk grandfather, who would sometimes engage me in dialogue to get me to develop my own understanding of the

world around me. At other times, he told me vivid stories about what it was like when he was a boy and how his elders taught him. I can still image him in an outer circle, listening to the inner circle of elders as they sat in council to reflect on the weighty issues of their time. Each would speak in turn, bringing a unique perspective or filling in what had been missed by the others. Together, they would build a common picture of the situation and, over time, come to a shared understanding of what action needed to be taken.

These conversations immersed younger listeners in a deep lineage stream, which flowed through generations and brought forward language, stories, history, ethics, science, cosmology, and governance within a self-determination view of human responsibility. All the work was indirect—conversation, decision making, community building, and teaching—and all of it emphasized the need for people to think and take responsibility for themselves. These values were carried forward and embedded in the ways my grandfather taught me, and I hope that I have found ways to bring them forward in the life I have lived in my non-Mohawk world.

I attempt to work within a living oral tradition in multiple ways. For example, I seek to use every interaction as an opportunity, live and in the moment, to disrupt my own and other people's inner habits of belief and thought as a way to see through them to something new. When introducing a subject or new idea, I ask people to form their own thoughts about it before I share my thinking. The ability to hold two thoughts at once and the cognitive dissonance that this often creates are key to finding new insight, a third possibility that is uniquely one's own.

I also limit the use of written materials because these can so easily supplant the living oral experience itself, and when I do share notes, I limit their circulation to those who are present and engaged in the discussion. We have many ways of tricking ourselves into relying on outside expertise, and referring to a text is one of the most common.

At all times, I discipline myself to remain anchored in deep lineage and philosophical traditions that have been tested and validated again and again by self-directing thinkers and handed down over generations. I have become more proficient at this practice over time, and it has rewarded me with immunization against facile pop psychology and humanist ideas and given me a more reliable base from which to evolve my thinking.

Together, these practices and others like them ensure that my teaching is tuned to activating self-directed learning—and make it unlikely that I will ever be mistaken for an expert, authority, or guru.

*Colgate South Africa*: To lead the transformation process, we set up a core team to take responsibility for the essence of the company and identify the evolutionary path that would express more of its potential into its markets and South Africa's changing society. A core team's role is to manage the boundary between the organization and its environment, setting and assessing the strategic direction and guiding decision-making processes in accordance with strategy. The core team acted as a council of elders, a concept that was deeply familiar to tribal South Africans. We invited participants from every part of the organization, without regard to where they fell within the old hierarchy, to create a circle that could reflect and create intelligence about the whole of the system. Our criteria for inviting them was that they be willing to think about the whole. My role was to be their resource, introducing questions, exercises, and practices that would invite them to examine and upgrade the sources of their thinking.

For example, we created a little ritual in which, before working on a particular subject, the team would talk together about the premises and beliefs they held about the subject and ask themselves where they got these ideas. This was a startlingly effective way to prepare them to take a fresh look. I also introduced the idea that the notes and written materials they received from me were not to be shared outside of the circle who had worked with them. They understood and respected the fact that this was not about protecting proprietary materials. It was about protecting *against* a return of the old external-authority corporate culture.

4. ***Form (or find) a developmental community.*** Leading fundamental change, going up against the broad consensus about how things ought to work, is no easy task. This is certainly true for anyone attempting to operate from the self-determination theory of knowledge, which upends almost every assumption around which our social institutions are currently organized. It is no accident that effective change leaders almost always

emerge from or gather around themselves communities of practice that operate from a shared paradigm, theory of knowledge, and set of practices. These friends and colleagues on a shared path help us to remember what we are trying to do, why it matters, and how important it is to take an approach that is congruent with our beliefs.

A developmental community continuously presents us with opportunities to evolve our thinking and our state of being, even as we invite those around us to evolve as well. Without such a community, we find ourselves alone in workplaces, classrooms, social groups, and media that arise out of paradigms that conflict with the one we seek to live from. The pressures to go along with the mainstream of social consensus are tremendous. Developmental communities enable us to sustain our will and to become increasingly effective regarding the change we are seeking to make. They do this by evolving a precise and nuanced language and a shared set of frameworks that support independent critical thinking and challenge the authority-based mental models that creep back into our minds without our conscious awareness.

*Colgate South Africa*: The cumulative effects of the many changes we implemented created a profound shift in company culture, and, as a result, a strong sense of community arose. Together, we were pioneering changes of utmost importance not only to Colgate's survival but to the future of the nation. This created impetus for a shared commitment to development that would grow potential in every member of the organization and thus create enduring benefits to their families, communities, and future places of employment. Inner and outer development was core to the collective ethos, and workers benefited from an environment that supported their conscious efforts to go beyond what had been conceivable in the past. They related to one another as partners in development and quickly extended this idea beyond the company to include suppliers, distributors, and other business stakeholders.

Colgate established a developmental infrastructure that included resourcing, reflection rituals, self-assessment practices, and many other capacity-building activities. Every team was charged with responsibility for calling on this infrastructure as needed to help them challenge and supersede their old thinking and evolve their effectiveness.

This community spirit was the first time-binding effect of our work, and it created the conditions that enabled the organization to engage consciously in its own evolution. Our process also built the time-binding capacity of individual workers, many of whom took their experiments in the arenas of self-directed development, product evolution, governance, and social change out of Colgate and extended them into their families, future employment, and lives in the townships.

5. ***Learn to see levels.*** A simple definition of time binding is *ongoing, multigenerational effort to understand the complex and continuously evolving nature of the universe.* One key to building this understanding is to learn how to discern order within complexity by means of nested or hierarchical mental structuring. For example, each of us is an individual nested within one or more larger social units—a family, group of friends, cohort, tribe— and this social unit is itself nested within a community, region, and set of cultural agreements.

These different levels are completely interdependent. Individual humans need social bonds and cultural contexts to survive and flourish, and social groupings are made up of and gain their character from the individuals within them. Moving mentally up the hierarchy reveals that each level has a different nature and order of complexity and that effecting change at higher levels requires increasingly sophisticated understanding.

As individuals, we humans are already complex beings, and thus knowing how to evolve ourselves is our most important foundational work. Learning to consciously evolve our societies and cultures and the institutions that sustain them is several levels up in order of complexity. Yet, by diligently working on our own capacity and the capacity of those who choose to join us, we can learn how to evolve these larger systems.

We can do this in a reliable and skillful way only when we have learned to discern the nested levels we are working on. I have used a relatively simple and concrete example to illustrate what I mean, but the idea of levels runs through everything I do. For example, the distinctions among external-authority, humanist, and self-determination theories of knowledge comprise a hierarchy that allows us to move up to increasing orders of creativity and effectiveness in thinking and understanding.

*Colgate South Africa*: Over the time we worked together at Colgate, Stelios Tsezos, the core team, and I used a number of *ordering* frameworks (hierarchical depictions of levels) to help everyone in the company manage the complexity of what we were trying to accomplish. One example was a three-part purpose framework that teams used to clarify and then remember why they were undertaking any activity. At the start of every project, team members first articulated the immediate result they intended to produce; second, they asked themselves what value this would deliver to customers; and third, they located these two levels within Colgate's overall strategy in relation to its industry and the South African context. Thinking this way enabled everyone to build a layered or nested understanding of every activity and quickly weeded out work that was meaningless or useless.

The three-part purpose framework was then reflected in a corresponding three-part thinking hierarchy (as opposed to a management hierarchy) that we established to guide our work. The *core team*, made up of diverse members from across the company, reflected on overall strategic direction within the industry and national economy that they were trying to evolve. A plethora of *market field teams* came up with unique ways to deliver new value to every part of the market. Every worker in the company was part of one or more field teams, and these were focused on understanding the lives and needs of specific customers, which allowed individual members to discover their promises beyond ableness. *Task teams* were set up to accomplish clear goals within specified time frames. They were responsible for translating new pursuits envisioned at the core and field team levels into on-the-ground projects. This three-tier framework was a practical way to help people learn, in real time and connected to real work, that they needed to take into account multiple levels of system and integrate them into all their efforts.

6. **Marry development to doing.** This practice points to the idea that time binding has a lot in common with certain kinds of spiritual discipline. Time binding requires us to be dedicated and faithful to the larger questions we have taken on, prioritizing them over the distractions and small pleasures that undermine our intentions to pursue a purposeful life. It also requires a kind of conscious ritualization of the activities we engage in at home,

in school, at work, and with our communities, using the vicissitudes and opportunities of life as raw material for the development of wisdom and conscientiousness in ourselves. From this perspective, *everything* we do offers an occasion for evolving the contributions we wish to make to the people we care about, the endeavors we are part of, and the world we live in.

To make self-development our way of being is a choice available to any of us, and it is critical to the purposes of time binding because it reins in our egotism. If we neglect self-development, the critical role of time binding can easily degrade into an exercise in personal aggrandizement and legacy building. This is not an attitude that is conducive to the humble self-reflection and self-awareness needed to deeply question received wisdom and contribute to the collective intelligence of the species. I understand that most of us long for recognition and acknowledgment, and in and of itself this is not necessarily a bad thing. But this longing can easily push us back into the role of expert and undermine the significance of what we are trying to create. Worldly recognition is not a motivation that harmonizes well with the rigorous demands of time binding.

*Colgate South Africa*: One reason I loved working with South African workers is the speed with which they moved to integrate what they were learning. We had a hard time keeping up with them and kept having to up the challenge and complexity of what we put before them. Unlike what I encountered in many other companies, where people treated ideas of regenerative practice as abstract and intellectually interesting, the South Africans made them concrete. They took everything we gave them and put it immediately to work, applying it on the factory floor, in meetings, and at home with their families.

When people tell me that building the capacity of people is too slow a way to work, I just shake my head. It's a culture problem, not a time problem. Colgate's workers built rituals around the new ways of thinking and working that they were trying to embody, and in this way they were able to make them part of daily life. Not a day went by when they were not dedicating time to practicing them.

In one particularly delightful example, they co-opted and repurposed two practices that had been implemented by an apartheid-era management team and that were universally loathed—check-ins and the 80-20 rule. They transformed their weekly check-ins into a reflection ritual in which they reported on the ways they were implementing the frameworks and processes they had learned and the differences this made. Suddenly, check-ins became places for developing consciousness and integrating and strengthening new practices.

They redefined the 80-20 rule (80 percent of outcomes derive from 20 percent of effort) as *80 percent of what you report on should be about work, 20 percent should be about how work was showing up at home and in communities.* This reinforced the idea that what they were learning could be meaningfully integrated into who they were becoming in every part of their lives. No wonder they could move so fast and create so much change in such a short amount of time: development really was a dimension of everything they did.

# Twelfth Intermezzo

As we move to *time binding*, the direction point in our tetrad, we bring forward the connections we made earlier between sourcing mind and systems intelligence. Having a source of direction helps us keep from collapsing into rote activity in pursuit of a goal. In this case, time binding reminds us of our efforts to actualize systems that are tied to the role of our species on Earth. It provides a reference point that spiritualizes any work we do on behalf of living systems while reining in our tendency toward anthropocentrism.

As time binders, human beings bring conscious understanding to the working of living systems and then use this consciousness to regenerate energy fields that enable other species to do their work of energy binding and space binding. Each generation is tasked with contributing to advancing and evolving our collective ability to carry out this human role. With the following set of questions, I invite you to reflect on time binding as a direction for your reading process.

## Capacity-Regenerating Questions

- It is challenging to develop and maintain awareness of the ways that cultures and subcultures shape our beliefs and experiences. Yet, to be self-determining requires making oneself aware of humanity's time-binding processes and critically examining our cultural assumptions about how living systems work. This is quite different from accepting conventional wisdom. On reflection, how is your reading experience influenced by an uncritical acceptance of received wisdom about how the universe works? Can you observe yourself behaving as part of a machinelike transfer of knowledge from one person to the next, from writer to reader?

- What would it be like to disengage from knowledge transfer, to read with active and critical inquiry, and to intentionally direct your reading process toward contributing to the evolution of human understanding?

- If you were to connect this thought with the important causes that you care about, how might you engage the groups you interact with in building will and committing to the work of time binding?

# Chapter Thirteen

# Long-Thought Practices

The *instrument* in a tetrad framework is the means and methods with which we work to accomplish an activity or project, consistently with the other three terms. In the Self-Determination Theory of Knowledge Tetrad, our instrument is *long-thought processes* (Figure 7).

*Time Binding*

*Sourcing Mind*                    *Systems Intelligence*

*Long-Thought*
*Processes*

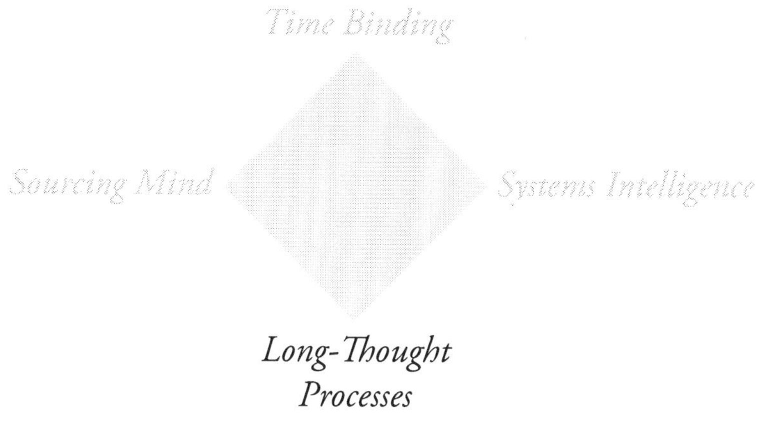

**Figure 7: Self-Determination Theory of Knowledge Tetrad:
Long-Thought Processes at the Instrument Point.**

My premise with regard to long-thought processes is that *people become wise and unlock their potential to contribute to the betterment of the world by faithfully surrendering themselves to the lifelong exploration of a profound question, rededicating themselves to going deeper each time they gain insight.* Long-thought processes are the means by which we consciously extend our minds into unfolding events (in contrast to occupying ourselves with repetitive or habitual mental activities). These processes are precisely the work of time binding.

Although time binding is generally thought to occur over generations and epochs, it can also be the work of individuals, which is apparent in the lives of great thinkers, artists, and spiritual leaders. For example, Mozart was a prodigy with extraordinary musical gifts. His contribution to the world derived not so much from his genius as it did from his lifelong drive to take music into the realm of the sublime. This pursuit, governed by his self-determining agency, continually pushed his work to higher levels; music he composed at the end of his life offered listeners an experience of the infinite.

Mozart's life demonstrates what unstinting dedication to a profound question looks like. Given his talent and accomplishment, he might have chosen to act as a musical tastemaker and expert composer of charming musical phrases—a star in the cultural firmament of the eighteenth century. Instead, he had the humility to know that more was possible, and this elevated his art to the highest degree. He plumbed his own depths and those of the musical traditions he worked within.

Mozart struggled constantly to find answers to the long-thought question he had set for himself, and he sacrificed everything nonessential to the exploration. He never settled for what he had already achieved, and he never lost his way. Following the direction he set for himself early on, he pressed forward into territory that neither he nor anyone else had visited before. This renunciation of self-satisfaction is characteristic of great artists, thinkers, sages, and saints. It is also available to any of us who genuinely wish to contribute something meaningful to the world with our lives. The key is to find a time-binding question that we care deeply enough about to work on for a lifetime, with all our inner resources and wealth.

## Six Practices for Developing Long-Thought Processes

Here is the principle I have drawn from my premise and used in my own work to remind myself of what we aim for when we put long-thought processes into practice: *Give yourself to a question—pursue your long-thought subject with ever-increasing precision and utility as you evolve its significance for humanity and the societies and ecosystems we inhabit.*

1. **1. Develop a semantic language.** By the time behaviorism came along, Western society had already gone a long way down the road of materialist bias. Behaviorists delivered the coup de grâce when they denied the existence or relevance of our inner lives. Thus, we have learned an *objective* language that attempts to describe our perceptions of the material world based on the evidence of our senses alone, and we have not developed a semantic language with which to frame the inner working of our minds.

I use the word *semantic,* which I borrow from Alfred Korzybski's work on general semantics, to emphasize meanings within the languages we speak. An objective language operates from the assumption that there are clear correlations between words and the phenomena they describe and that these correlations are shared and understood by most of the people who share the language. A familiar and recognizable language can be used to accurately and unambiguously transmit objective ideas in ways that are uniformly received and understood.

But objective language, which is an outward-facing instrument of the senses with a bias toward action, is inadequate for the development of agency, self-directed thinking, and consciousness. It cannot address the fact that our perceptions and interpretations of reality are strongly influenced by inner states and motivations, and thus that the ideal of perfectly clear communication is virtually unattainable. It also ignores and undermines many of the most powerful dimensions of human intelligence, which come into play when we seek to look beyond surface phenomena.

Semantic language addresses these shortfalls by adopting vocabulary, word choice, and syntax that pattern themselves on the processes out of which material phenomena arise. That is, we use semantic language to trigger the imaging capacity of the mind and build interior experience of the working of entities and systems and the purposes they serve. Semantic language does not seek to transmit a description of material existence but instead to generate or regenerate dynamic images of forces at play in the workings of things. Like many of the sentences in this book, semantic language is not immediately accessible. It can only be understood by a mind that has formed an image of processes at work. It often strikes listeners as a little odd and indirect or repetitive because its purpose is to bypass any belief that we know what words mean. In my experience, it is a terrifically powerful instrument for unlocking neglected human potentialities.

The inner dimension of work, which John Watson categorically dismissed, becomes accessible only in semantic language, which enables people to deepen their thinking through time and thus to build genuinely new understanding. This is a long-thought capability that has been degraded by generations of behaviorist conditioning, even though it is necessary for creation of the changes that foster evolution of organizations and societies. This is why we need to do the hard work it will take to rebuild it.

*Colgate South Africa*: A primary way that we built capability to use semantic language was to have teams develop purpose statements for every important meeting. In each case, they would first develop a statement using objective language. Then they would rewrite it in semantic language. The contrast was instrumental in reminding team members of the difference, which they underscored by giving objective language an unflattering title, *the colonialist way.*

Here is a simple example. Among our myriad teams was one whose responsibility was to make decisions about funding projects proposed by the market field teams based on their members' promises beyond ableness. On an occasion when a project team submitted a proposal, the venture capital team's purpose statement, written in objective language, looked something like this:

> To make a decision about the viability of a market field team proposal based on Colgate's funding framework and the ability of the team to deliver on the project, and to do this in an open and relaxed way that builds clarity and confidence for all involved team members.

Rewritten in semantic language, it might have looked like this:

> To come to a shared understanding that reveals to everyone involved the self-evidently right thing to do. To do this in a

way that realizes the essences of both the market team and the customers their proposal intends to serve, such that the potentials of the team, its customers, and our shared market strategy is developed.

Note that the second version is longer and may seem harder to access—a demonstration of what I mean when I say that to understand semantic language requires imaging something at work.

In practice, we would dedicate the beginning of a meeting to discussing the language of the semantic version of a purpose statement until it became alive and meaningful for all present, raising the level of energy and will available for the group to do its work. The semantic version of the statement focused on a project's inner meaning and its intended contribution to the development of capability.

2. ***Resource the quality of thinking.*** One reason for engaging in a long-thought process is that it forces us to develop ourselves. To make a meaningful contribution to a worthy subject, and thus to participate in the evolutionary work of time binding, depends on our ability to move past the shallow thinking and mental models that inhibit creative insight. Resourcing creates the conditions for this to occur.

Although not impossible, it is difficult to resource oneself. Thus, it is helpful to belong to a developmental community, where people are learning to resource one another. In the many organizations I worked with over the years, the magic really began to happen when people got excited about the possibility of serving as resources for one another's thinking and personal development. That was when the evolution of thinking became an ordinary and integrated aspect of daily work and life.

As a practice, we need to be willing to be resourced and to resource others if we are to gain proficiency. When resourcing, we learn to step into a distinctive mode of mental processing, one that draws on other practices that I have described. A resource helps others to examine how their thinking is sourced, for example by using frameworks coupled with Socratic questioning to test and upgrade the quality and coherence of what gets generated.

The aim of resourcing is to enable people to take full responsibility for themselves as the sources of ideas whose validity they have tested in experience and which they are keeping open for further examination and revision. This returns to people the freedom and capacity to self-direct, allowing them to evolve who they are and how they think. It is an awesome responsibility and requires humility and dedication from the resource, who must honestly believe in and care about the self-directing potential of the people they work with.

*Colgate South Africa:* In our reimagining and re-creation of Colgate South Africa, many roles that had been highly stratified, such as manager and supervisor, simply disappeared, to be replaced by roles that were more consistent with the newly envisioned potential of the company. Our new roles included, for example, core team member, market field team member, and project steward. Within these roles, everyone was expected to become ever better at managing and thinking for themself. One newly created role that some people felt drawn to pursue was that of resource. It was understood that everyone had operational work to do, but a small number of people, approximately 5 percent of the workforce, wanted to make themselves available to be called on whenever resourcing was required. Their task was to help individuals and teams apply frameworks in order to upgrade the quality of their thinking, and they became proficient in the work and much appreciated for taking it on. One of my roles then became fast-tracking the development of capabilities among this group, because they had such a profound multiplier effect on the performance of everyone else in the company.

3. ***Schedule recurring rituals of development.*** Like every other dimension of the self-determination theory of knowledge, long-thought processes are strengthened and accelerated when undertaken within a developmental community that shares a ritual of regular, recurring meetings to build capability in its members. These developmental rituals are one of the key instruments that I introduced to help companies transform themselves into developmental organizations. They immerse us in a dynamic and challenging environment where we can expect to put our thinking to the test with people we work with naturally in daily activities. They also provide an arena to develop agency and disciplined thinking and to raise the quality of our ideation *for the purpose* of making beneficial contributions to the work we share. Under these exposed and transparent conditions, it

is not only our thinking that we need to elevate, but also our state of being and the exercise of our will.

I call such sessions *rituals* because their purpose is to grow a self-directing thinking culture, and for this reason, they need to invite people to engage in ways that go beyond the purely functional and mundane. Unlike conventional education for information or skills transfer, these ritualized gatherings approach development as an ongoing and iterative process, where ideas are reencountered again and again, deepening each time we engage with them. In this way, rituals of development exemplify the continual evolution of thinking about a subject that is a necessary aspect of long-thought processes.

*Colgate South Africa*: I lived in the United States when I worked with Colgate, and we had to be clever about how we managed the time I could be in-country with the Colgate workers. I traveled there every six weeks for a mega-session that included the core team, up to half of every market field team, and a mix of customers and suppliers. The sessions had a strongly ritualized feel to them because we always worked on how to raise and sustain will and manage our states of being as integral to our capability to function well.

Team members knew that their will was deeply connected to some customer node that they were trying to serve. Every time they generated a breakthrough in how to work on behalf of this node, they saw their will go through the roof. At the same time, managing state of being was critical to operating successfully in the high-pressure environment that was South Africa at the time. These learnings were then brought by the resources into weekly team meetings, which in turn became developmental rituals, engaging everyone who had not been able to attend the big session and putting the new ideas generated there into practice immediately. The effect was a continuous building of energy, as previously boring weekly work meetings were transformed into rituals that tapped into a sacred responsibility for the well-being of their customers, communities, and nation.

4. **Work from lived experience.** The purpose of a long-thought process is to generate thinking that is continually deepening and becoming more grounded. It is not about rote recycling of what others have said or done.

This means that we all need to gain confidence and ableness in working by reflecting on our lived experience, which is the best source for expanding and deepening understanding.

Lived experience in and of itself does not necessarily yield insight, which depends on our ability to use conscious reflection to examine or become discerning about our experiences. I use the word *reflection* to mean something particular: the ability to look closely at something happening within us, bringing focus and precision to understand it better. By *examination*, I mean the careful discernment that allows me to evaluate the source and quality of my thinking. By *consciousness*, I mean the divided awareness that allows me to observe and manage myself as I engage in a process.

Taken together, these capabilities represent a method that puts us in an excellent position to harvest the wealth of insight that can be gained from an experience. We can then use these insights to formulate premises about the meaning of our experiences and test these premises by engaging with new experiences.

*Colgate South Africa*: When I first arrived at Colgate South Africa, people would report out on the work done by their small groups. I could tell something was off because these reports were so desperately flat in tone and spirit. I thought about it and realized that people were not speaking from their own experience, and so their sharing felt empty and inauthentic. I implemented a practice that included only speaking one's own experience of what happened in one's groups, and I made a point of asking follow-up questions for reflection.

For example, if a team had been assigned the task of improving a production process to deliver better results for customers, I might ask one member to report on how his understanding of improvement in this context had been upgraded as he was working (reflection). Then I might ask him to examine the source of his ideas and how he might lift them up to a different level (examination). Finally, I might ask him to speak about what was happening regarding his ability to manage his own thinking process and state of being as I quizzed him in front of the group (consciousness). In an exchange like this, by being openly thoughtful about his own experience, the worker would have been contributing to growing the quality of thinking possible for everyone present.

The change was enthusiastically embraced, and the improvements in our sessions and the business were immediate. Suddenly, report-outs were yielding real and meaningful content that was of value to everyone in the room, and we were watching people evolve their thinking live and in front of us. I suspect that within the tribal cultures that most of these participants grew up in, they were expected to speak from their own perspectives when addressing their communities. To them, this felt like a much more natural way to contribute. Ever since then, I have insisted that people speak from their own experience when doing collective work.

5. ***Examine first.*** There was a moment early in my career when I woke up to the uncomfortable realization that I was absorbing ideas from sources around me that I respected. If something I heard or read appeared valuable, it went into my basket of tricks, to be pulled out the next time I needed a good idea about a particular subject. Once I became aware of this pattern, I could see it everywhere, in my history and education and in the people around me.

We absorb or borrow ideas without testing them, let alone regenerating them in our own experience and thinking processes. We also reject ideas if they disagree with our currently held beliefs and assumptions, again without testing them. Ever since that moment of realization, I have diligently tried to live by this principle: *neither adopt nor reject the ideas of others without conscious discernment.* Instead, suspend your preexisting judgments and attachments and immerse yourself fully into an experience of how the meaning and implications of these ideas work within you (in other words, no pusillanimous toe-dipping). Then rigorously examine their underlying premises and frameworks to understand the paradigms from which they are sourced.

For some reason, this principle is hard to live up to when we read, particularly when the author seems credible and their argument is persuasive. This is why I began to experiment in my last book, *Indirect Work*, with *intermezzos* that would interrupt the tendency of readers to either accept or critique what I was saying, rather than really think about it. Examination builds the capacity for discernment, for making fine distinctions about the value or relevance of ideas. It also builds the capacity to move an idea forward, refining and evolving it as part of the overall work involved in stewarding a long-thought process.

*Colgate South Africa:* Inherent in the apartheid system was that Black South Africans were neither invited nor allowed to think for themselves. Their task was to do what they were told to do by their employers and the government. So, we introduced a process to Colgate workers for building their capability to think and speak for themselves. They loved this because, like so many of our processes, it violated a fundamental taboo of apartheid culture.

We asked all workers to keep a journal at work in which to submit written texts to close examination. I brought them articles and book excerpts, and they brought in articles that they wanted to think about. They worked through the texts slowly, reflecting as they went. They then divided a sheet of paper in half from top to bottom. On the left-hand side, they made notes about the text, using a framework to assess what was missing or incomplete in the author's perspective or thinking. On the right-hand side, they evaluated the quality and source of their own thinking.

This simple, contrarian exercise, repeated every time we got together, began to build very rigorous critical-thinking skills across the company, preparing workers to take on increasingly complex responsibilities within Colgate and in their communities. The workers themselves reported to me that they could tell that they were getting smarter. I laughed and shared a little of my story, reminding them that I had been repeatedly told by my father that I was stupid and would never amount to anything, a family's version of apartheid messaging. What had saved me was that I was a contrarian by nature (though not a condemning one). The impulse to challenge and see something larger than whatever I was told guaranteed that I would always have an inner drive and method to evolve my intelligence.

6. ***Become imperturbable.*** A long-thought question requires us to push ourselves beyond what we know, are certain of, and feel comfortable with. It embodies a conscious intention to challenge and destabilize ourselves so that we can move our minds and perceptions into uncharted territory. For most of us, this kind of uncertainty is deeply disturbing and will tend

to evoke default responses, such as giving up or becoming hypersensitive about what we believe others think of us.

To do long-thought work, we must become imperturbable so that the challenges we will inevitably encounter will not knock us off-center. In my experience, the best way to build imperturbability is to be part of a developmental community whose culture includes an agreement to work on those things that perturb us. Membership in a working community in and of itself is likely to be disturbing because we almost always find that certain people or situations will be disagreeable or incomprehensible to us. Rather than avoiding this social discomfort, we learn to step into it, growing our ability to manage our state so as to advance the larger purposes we hope to serve.

Over time, we find that we can handle increasing levels of discomfort and unpredictability without being distracted or undermined, learning to bring a stable focus and demeanor that lifts the spirit and focus of those around us. Even those of us who are temperamental, passionate, or prone to quick reactions can develop this basic capacity for steadiness in the face of volatile conditions.

*Colgate South Africa*: When forming the core team at Colgate, we invited people from across the company who we thought might be up for the challenge. At the beginning of our first meeting, Stelios Tsezos stood up to give the prospective members an idea of what to expect. "My friends," he announced,

> you are not being invited to be leaders in any conventional sense of the word. On the contrary, you are being invited to become humble servants of your coworkers, your company, your nation, and everything we hope to create together. Carol's role will be to disrupt you, to shake up your beliefs and thought patterns so that you can truly do what you say you want to do. In every session, she will embarrass you in front of the whole group, but please understand that she does this because she cares about you. She will ask you to listen deeply to the people you disagree with or dislike, because they bring something to the table that is important for you to understand. She will ask you to do deep personal development work, even

though this is not customary in business settings, because it will be necessary if you are to undertake the profound social and business changes we are aiming for. In the end, you will get to a place where you cannot be embarrassed or knocked off-center, because you will have built a deep capacity for imperturbability.

Please know this is difficult for Carol. It is the opposite of what we expect to do when we want to make friends. But if you choose to commit to being part of this core team and doing this work, I believe that you will end up loving her as much as she loves you. Meanwhile, don't forget that it is not just about having Carol disrupt us. After all, she is teaching us how to do it for ourselves and each other.

I have selected a framework that I am going to be using to help me discern when I am being *reactive*, when I am operating from my *ego*, and when, by contrast, I am being *purposeful*. This is how I will be improving my ability to manage myself through the ups and downs of our work together.

With this moving and truthful statement, Tsezos launched a core team that ended up creating miraculous change. Many core team members later described this work as the most transformative experience of their lives; it provided an inner compass and steadiness that would allow them to play leadership roles in the emergence of a new South Africa.

# Thirteenth Intermezzo

When we bring *long-thought processes,* the instrument in our tetrad, together with sourcing mind, systems intelligence, and time binding, we are able to see the means we can deploy to do the work we have laid out for ourselves. Long-thought processes are characterized by deep commitment to disrupting our own certainties; without them, we would think the same thoughts over and over again, forever. One could say that they elevate disruption to an art form: with them, we try on new formulations, listen to voices we may have missed or discounted, and prevent ourselves from becoming too comfortable or sure of what we think. This enables us to continually bring fresh perspectives and generate fresh insights into our long-thought questions.

With the following questions, I invite you to reflect on long-thought processes as an instrument for your reading.

## Capacity-Regenerating Questions

- If I have done my job well, this book has been effective at disrupting your existing reading habits and patterns. This disruption will become more meaningful when you connect it to what is deeply compelling to you. Consider the causes that feel most important to you, those that are crucial in terms of planetary evolution (for example, civil rights or preventing habitat loss). Where do you see the use of repetitive or uncreative thinking and divisive rhetoric? In yourself and your family? Among your colleagues? In public discourse?

- How can you use the ideas presented in this book to disrupt those old messages and ways of thinking? What are some of the bigger questions that lie behind the causes you care about? What cause and question are most meaningful to you? Where are you drawn to commit yourself?

- Review the six practices in chapter 13 and the six disciplines described in chapter 7. Create a plan for how you will go to work on disrupting yourself and others when it comes to your long-thought question and the causes most important to you.

# CHAPTER FOURTEEN

# AN AFTERWORD ON MAINTAINING INTEGRITY

Readers may have noticed that the practices described in chapters 9 through 13, when taken together as a system, indicate a complete transformation in perspective from the behaviorist and humanist approaches that have dominated every aspect of our lives over the last century. This is why I insist that people not cherry-pick the practices that feel most familiar or comfortable, mixing them with behaviorist or other methods to create an epistemological Frankenstein monster. In and of themselves, the practices are not what is important—they are only a sampling of the many approaches that I have learned or invented as a developmental process designer.

What really matters are the underlying perspective and philosophy because these commit us to the development of a self-determination orientation and capability in ourselves and the people we serve. Once a person has grasped this, they can continue to generate new practices that are consistent and of a piece with those I have described here. These new practices will be needed as antidotes to the thousands of behaviorist practices that have rooted themselves so deeply into our social consensus.

## This *Is* Doable

I hope to have clearly demonstrated that it is possible to create the conditions for broad adoption of the self-determination theory of knowledge and the mental disciplines based on it. I have demonstrated it to myself over the years with the developmental processes that I brought to diverse working communities around the world. *Help people think for themselves* has been the consistent theme in all my efforts to elevate work design, business strategy, leadership development, and community governance. Self-directed thinking is the only basis for building the personal agency and systems intelligence required to regenerate our social and economic systems and reverse our path to self-destruction.

The fact that epistemological change has been my underlying theme of study and practice is not just an interesting footnote. It informs everything I have done and said in the long course of my work. Epistemological change is central, representing a profound and total shift in outlook and approach across cultures, institutions, and enterprises. What I have presented in this and all my prior books arises from a foundational and consistent worldview and ultimately only makes sense when understood through the lens of this worldview. The multiple frameworks, practices, and examples that I have offered are not freestanding and independent tools to be separated out and used at will. Rather, they are expressions of a coherent technology; they have the power to create transformative change, but only if they work together.

I have said this in a variety of ways over the years because it is fundamental. You could put every idea I have presented here directly into action and still fail to create genuine change, particularly at the epistemological level, because this is not about action. It is about change inside of each of us, in the ways we perceive and understand the world and our roles and responsibilities within it. Put another way, *indirect work* is *inner work*, and the most profound inner work that we can do is to transform our theory of knowledge.

The practices I have suggested arose from my engagement with the long-thought question that I have focused on since I was a college student. That question has led me to experiment with ways to grow the capacity in people to consciously think for themselves. All my suggested processes work together as a whole to grow this capacity, but one must be willing to be changed by them. They are an entrance into a different way of working and thinking rather than a set of nifty techniques to fill out one's toolbox. They are representative of a much larger set of possible practices, many of which remain to be discovered by my readers as they engage in their own long-thought processes.

Over the years, experience has revealed to me several pitfalls that people are likely to encounter in their attempts to understand and integrate these ideas into their lives and work. There is the temptation to pick and choose, to mix and match, which violates the wholeness of this approach. There is the widespread notion that these are techniques that can be picked up in a weekend workshop or training, when in fact they reflect a new pattern for living that must be cultivated and evolved over years. And there is the belief that people become virtuous and wise through strict observance of externally constructed codes of ethics and behavior, but this neglects the will and spirit that could be uniquely expressed in each human being but which remain fallow and undeveloped.

## Don't Pick and Choose—Don't Mix and Match

The self-direction theory of knowledge operates at an entirely different level than either the external-authority or the humanist theory. It emerges from an entirely different worldview. When we embrace practices from one of the other-directed lower levels, we reinforce those levels and cause the mind to operate within their rules and assumptions. For example, it is self-defeating to play the role of expert when encouraging people to be self-directed in their thinking and to forgo authority. It is absurd to tell people how to self-direct by laying out the well-researched best practices revealed to us by experts. Don't laugh! This kind of confusion around intentions and levels of paradigm is so common as to be nearly universal, and it prevents us from embracing a self-determination approach to create social and institutional change.

I think that there are several sources for this confusion. The most important comes from the fact that most of us lack any real exposure to and experience with the idea of levels or orders. I see people embracing the three theories of knowledge that I have explored here as though they were basically distinct but equivalent options, to be put on and taken off like sets of clothes, depending on what the situation demands. From this point of view, taking a little from authoritative sources, adding a bit of humanism, and finishing with a touch of self-determination for excitement is the best of all worlds!

Unfortunately, this is what magpies do when they collect shiny bits of stuff. It misses the unshiny point that these different epistemologies are incommensurate, that the potentials they enable are of different orders. The capacity to think for ourselves cannot be cultivated by asking others to tell us how to think, no matter how benign or enlightened these others might be. We must climb up to a different level of discipline and self-accountability to achieve the potential for mental independence and creativity available from the self-determination theory of knowledge. We must learn to discern and set aside thoughts and language that arise from the lower-level theories and develop the capacity to think for ourselves.

A corollary to the inability to see differences in level is an instinct to be inclusive and inoffensive in our approach, which ultimately comes out of our desires to adhere to norms and belong to a community. If someone badly needs us to step into the role of expert or wise counselor, wouldn't it be unkind to deny them? Maybe. But if we are seriously attempting to help people shed their conditioning and develop self-direction and independent thinking, we must restrain ourselves. We can no longer play the role of expert or benevolent guide to the truth. The hard fact is that assuming any person or group of people cannot learn to do their own thinking is condescending; genuine inclusivity requires that we place this demand on them as well as on ourselves. Conditioning does not need protection or inclusion; what we are responsible for nurturing is the innate intelligence and distinctive, self-generated perspectives that lie within each of us.

One other source of confusion comes from the fact that some of the ideas associated with a self-determination theory of knowledge sound good. People want to be associated with them—"Thinking for myself? I'm for that!"—and so they split off fragments to use as slogans or advertising copy. This kind of borrowing is well-intended, but no less fragmenting and destructive to the underlying integrity of the approach. The appropriate relationship with these ideas is commitment to the *whole* of the theory of knowledge and the worldview from which they gain their meaning and power. Without this wholeness, we are left only with fragments incapable of producing genuine or lasting change.

Two practices that I have adopted to help me maintain integrity may be useful to my readers. The first is to remind myself often that I am one person in a long lineage, not the original source of the ideas presented here. This helps me manage my ego and keeps me from getting overly hooked by praise or criticism. As much as possible, I try to relate as what I am, a member of a large lineage school; interactions with colleagues and fellow learners keep my thinking whole and my understanding always evolving. In particular, *I seek to focus on the lineage I belong to rather than the legacy I am creating.* This has proven to be beneficial as I approach the end of my life. It helps me maintain my active engagement with people and initiatives I care deeply about while guarding me against narrowing my attention to my own accomplishments.

The second practice is always to do this lineage work within the context of developmental communities, which helps rein in any longing for self-satisfaction. Responsibility for a change process in a company or community requires me to stay focused on the people whose development I am serving. An example of systems-actualization in action, *the aim is always to elevate the contribution of an entire organization to the betterment of life for its beneficiaries.* A systems-actualizing context enables me to remain purposeful and allows me to test the effectiveness of the overall work that I am doing. It also reinforces the importance of avoiding any lower-order practices that might undermine people's increasing ability to be self-managing and self-evaluating.

## Layering, Not Atomizing

Learning has two basic purposes: to transfer knowledge into the mind or, by generating and extending understanding, to develop the capacity of the mind to do its own thinking. Each of these purposes has its own methods. One is the process of breaking reality into digestible fragments that can be learned piece by piece. The other is a self-generated process that continuously circles a subject or question, approaching it again and again for an increasingly whole, dimensional, nuanced, and deep understanding.

Knowledge transfer, which has its origins in the external-authority theory, is very effectively accomplished by methods that are well-established, proven, and familiar to most of us from our educational upbringing. Begin with standardized materials that have been organized by subject matter, tested with research, and vetted by experts. Introduce these materials in intense bursts of focused learning around discrete topics, where one topic is added to another and another. Encourage participants, trainees, or students to review lessons in order to increase the amount of knowledge absorbed; confirm absorption with testing or hypothetical experience. Emphasize individual learning, grading students on how well they have taken in and retained information and rewarding them for success. Once a student has mastered the material and learned to apply it, move them on to new material that builds in a linear progression on what they have already learned.

The result of this process is to condition learners to look outside of themselves for what they need, which is precisely why this kind of education played such an important role in the colonization of local communities around the world. The disjointedness, linearity, and intensity of the process prevents reflection and therefore ownership of one's own thoughts. Information is presented in digestible chunks or batches rather than in the kind of slow and continuous process that allows one to integrate and weave knowledge into a whole, layered understanding over the course of an entire lifetime,

The alternative theory of knowledge, which I have called *self-determination*, adopts the long-thought approach used by great thinkers throughout time. It recognizes that an engagement with what is important is a necessarily iterative process, requiring continuous rethinking supported by some kind of framework. In this theory, learning occurs by slowly encompassing and elaborating, layering and questioning, reflecting and revealing.

A long-thought process seeks to reveal the innate complexity and wholeness inherent in a subject rather than oversimplifying it. It acknowledges that there is an inner dimension of learning that develops a mind capable of discerning its biases and limitations and acknowledging that these can easily contaminate the thinking process. This deconditions our tendency to borrow conventional wisdom without question. It also reverses generations of delegitimization imposed by conquerors on their colonized subjects. We become able to relearn our methods of understanding and reclaim the joy of discovering what there is to discover; we are no longer controlled by an externally imposed imperative to study for the test. Growing wiser through self-directed effort is its own reward, one far more meaningful than any credentials and accolades supplied by an authoritarian institution.

From the moment this distinction became apparent to me, I have dedicated my life to creating developmental processes that enable people to learn how to create and contribute from within themselves, engaging their own intelligence and care for the world around them. I have kept this commitment fresh for myself so that I, too, am continually discovering and reexamining my beliefs and assumptions. As I described earlier in this book, the long-thought inquiry I pursue asks how we grow motivation and consciousness regarding our role as humans on Earth. I regularly use a stop exercise that helps me reconnect with this inquiry: *never do my work the same way twice.*

Every time I lead a workshop or design a change process, I come at it from a new angle, a new idea about what this could be about and what it could accomplish, and thus how to introduce it. I do not create lessons and recycle them endlessly because that would cause my thinking to become rote. I use ideas or frameworks that I have developed in the past, but I am always uncovering new perspectives on what I think I know or understand. I am a discoverer, not an expert, working continuously to extend the boundaries of my current understanding. And because I am transparent about this, participants in the events I design experience themselves as cocreators rather than students. Through my long-thought process, self-directed by my stop exercise, I have been able to watch myself get smarter over the years, along with the people I have worked with.

## DON'T CONVINCE, DEVELOP!

*No More Gold Stars* is about helping people learn to think for themselves, and I believe it is necessary because so many of us have been trained out of this fundamental capacity. We are born with innate creativity, filled with the potential to become independent and innovative human beings who can exercise discernment and critical thinking. But given the philosophies and practices of our child-rearing, educational, and professional institutions, it can be difficult to manifest this potential. As a result, most of us are conditioned to look to others to do our thinking for us. We seek out those who seem credible, thorough, and persuasive, but were we to closely examine the quality and sourcing of their thinking, we would find that it, too, is borrowed.

The consequences of this conditioning are beginning to shake the foundations of democracies around the world. Many people recognize the growing threat of authoritarianism, but most of them are trying to address it through the wrong theory of knowledge. They work hard to convince people to be good citizens, reduce their energy consumption, address inequality, participate in electoral politics, and be inclusive of people who are different from them. What they do not recognize is that in the act of convincing, they are participating in and continuing to strengthen the underlying expert-driven theory of knowledge that created the problem in the first place.

The possibility of thinking for ourselves is innate, but it must be developed, and this development is a long, slow process to be undertaken throughout a lifetime. Such a process is both more likely and more rewarding when it is shared in community and supported by the comradeship of people who also embrace the challenge of learning how to do their own thinking. When we are not engaged developmentally, there is a strong likelihood that we will become aimless and inadequately discerning about the ideas and beliefs that we adopt. This makes us susceptible to cultish ideologies and authoritarianism.

Over the years, I have created a framework based on an idea conceived of by Armenian philosopher George Ivanovich Gurdjieff in his effort to make sense of the horrors of World War II. The framework helps me better understand the social dynamics related to the relative lack of thinking development in the United States. I conceptualize it as a hierarchy of possibilities for human development (Figure 8).

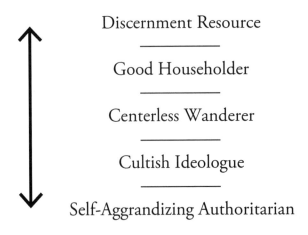

Discernment Resource

Good Householder

Centerless Wanderer

Cultish Ideologue

Self-Aggrandizing Authoritarian

**Figure 8: Levels of Human Development Framework**

Of particular concern to me are the *centerless wanderers*, people who have chosen to avoid or have not encountered opportunities for their own development. Wanderers look to others for guidance because they lack a *center*—the inner sense of what is right and what it means to be in touch with oneself. The natural result of institutionalized conditioning, they are malleable, subject to their own whims and preferences, and swayed by the strong beliefs of others. The feeling of having no center, of rootlessness, can be painful or even frightening, and it often leads wanderers to seek out a group or leader that will make them feel safe. Thus, they are susceptible to cultish ideologies, such as religious fanaticism, cults of personality or fandom, devotion to various sorts of conspiracy theory, and revolutionary militancy.

When a wanderer falls down a rabbit hole of unfounded belief, they lose contact with reality and willfully adopt a worldview that purports to provide answers, to make sense of phenomena that otherwise seem overwhelming and unintelligible. Cults are attractive because they offer a sense of belonging and a set of fixed beliefs about what is true, along with a promise to take care of their members. In exchange, they discourage self-examination, critical thinking, exploration of their fundamental premises, and experiences that might cause members to doubt these premises. Membership is enforced by shaming, threats of banishment, and even physical restraint. In many cases, cults also require proselytizing, both to recruit new members and to impose their version of the truth through media manipulation or legislation.

Whereas wanderers are swayed first in one direction and then another by persuasive ideas and charismatic leaders, *cultish ideologues* turn the content of their thinking entirely over to *authoritarian* individuals and systems. These authoritarians are willing to dehumanize others for their own benefit. When this is the result of a conscious choice, we characterize it as evil. But even if we have no conscious intent to do evil, when we unconsciously enjoy privileges that come at the expense of the material well-being, dignity, or aspirations of others, we are participants in an authoritarian process. It is useful to bear this in mind when we are tempted to label others as evil.

While someone who has consciously chosen to be a self-aggrandizing authoritarian is probably incorrigible, there is always a hope that wanderers, and even cult members, can develop a sense of their own center and learn to think for themselves. Because self-determination is so important for the healthy functioning of democratic societies, it is imperative that people at the higher levels of development—the *good householders* and *discernment resources*—dedicate significant energy to this purpose.

Discernment resources are people who believe that life has more value when it is infused with meaning. They therefore believe in and engage with inner work, for the sake of themselves and others. This provides them with a strong center, grounded in a self that is continually seeking its own evolution with regard to what it has chosen to serve. They carry their share of the load in the groups and communities they belong to, taking responsibility for themselves to avoid placing emotional or economic burdens on others. Because they are dedicated to systems-actualization, they seek to manifest increased capacity for self-direction in the people and systems they encounter. They believe that the quickest and most effective way to create profound change is to return agency and the capacity for good decision making to people, institutions, and living systems.

In this regard, they are different from good householders, the people that I describe as well-intended. Good householders have a clear sense of what it means to be good people and seek equanimity by pursuing consistently responsible and ethical lives. They feel a sense of duty to serve humanity or the planet and will gladly contribute their life energy to a cause or purpose that feels important. This also gives them a center, but it comes from a set of morals and ethics established by a psychological, philosophical, or religious school of thought.

Good householders seek to serve those who are in need, the wanderers and ideologues, but do so by trying to convince them to adopt a better path. They spend huge amounts of energy trying to persuade the public of the need for recycling and conserving, tolerance, and equitable sharing of benefits. But they fail to see that even though the message might be very different, in their advocacy they are replicating the social change methods of cultish ideologues. By insisting on the rightness of their cause, they fail to notice that they have not addressed the critical need of a wanderer or cult member to find their own center. No matter how good their thinking seems to be, getting others to think like them will always prevent them from thinking for themselves.

Although the shared intention of good householders may be benign—a society that works for everyone—their methods can easily become degenerative. Advocacy might achieve incremental improvements, but it also almost always fosters resistance. Thus the pendulum ultimately swings toward opposition to the desired change. At the same time, failure to address the underlying need inevitably results in a younger generation as susceptible as its elders to propaganda, social control, conspiracy theories, and cultism. And as a result of failure to develop self-aware, self-directed thinkers, well-intended efforts to correct current problems set the stage for yet another swing of the pendulum, again reversing what little progress has been made.

And so we come back around to where we started. The work of evolving society and the way that humans inhabit our planet cannot be accomplished through behavioral conditioning, role modeling, advocacy, or regulatory control. Direct methods may produce temporary results, but they leave intact our collective failure to develop discernment, independent thought, creativity, and commitment to time-binding endeavors. To reverse this failure requires an indirect and epistemological approach that rebuilds our commitment to individual self-determination. This will require a revolution in the ways we raise children, educate ourselves, manage work, and shape the social and legal infrastructures by which we govern ourselves.

As I approach the end of my life, I have great hope that we are on the cusp of just such a revolution. I pray that it will happen in good time.

# FINALE

It can be hard to avoid accepting and absorbing ideas without first examining their content and relevance to one's lived experience. The *No More Gold Stars* intermezzos were an attempt to disrupt your reading experience. But of course, in the long run it is up to you to become your own disruptor. This last set of questions invites you to create an ongoing disruption process for all your reading, or even for all your mental activities in general.

## CAPACITY-REGENERATING QUESTIONS

- Did you find yourself chafing at having to slow down your reading to work with the intermezzos? How did you respond?

- Which intermezzos did you find most helpful? Or which did you have the most patience for? What worked for you and what did these intermezzos enable you to manage in your reading process?

- What regular disruptions will you create to make your reading more intentional and self-directed going forward? What signals or clues can you watch for that will alert you to the need to read or listen in a more conscious and critical way?

- If relevant, what similar disruptions might you use to regenerate your writing practice? How does your writing relate to your reading?

- Will you introduce disruptions to other mental practices? How will you make them regular? For example, what might occur if, regularly throughout the day, you interrupted your train of thought? Would this make a beneficial contribution to managing function, being, and will?

# Appreciation and Indebtedness

As I bring my seventh book to completion, I want once again to thank my writing and editing team. First, my unbounded appreciation for Ben Haggard, my long-time co-creative partner, who has made it possible for me to author six books and multiple papers. He plays the role of developmental editor, helping to ensure that ideas are clear and compellingly conveyed. He walks with me chapter by chapter, joining my effort to maintain the right level of paradigm as I translate my thoughts into words. He strengthens my voice on the page, reshaping my words to sharpen them and make them accessible to readers. He never fails to find the precise representations to evoke images of living systems at work. I could not have become the author I aspired to be without him.

I am also grateful to Kit Brewer, who has worked on every one of my books and many of my other publications. She has taught me much about the art and craft of writing. Out of compassion for the poor reader, she takes my upside-down sentences and paragraphs and my tangled diction and syntax and makes them right, placing commas where they belong and removing dashes where they don't. More than a decade of working with her has deepened my appreciation for the interconnections between precision in thinking and precision in articulation.

I am indebted to the team at Book Launchers, who manage cover design, printing, e-book formatting, and marketing on my behalf. More than just a production team, they have consistently encouraged me with their warmth and enthusiastic support.

# INDEX

## A

actualize 99, 106, 161, 169

agency 4, 13, 15, 41, 42, 44, 45, 46, 63, 64, 77, 78, 79, 80, 93, 98, 109, 114, 122, 126, 138, 149, 172, 173, 176, 186, 194

Alfred Korzybski 57, 158, 173

assessment 12, 63, 104, 137, 138, 164

authoritarian 9, 16, 26, 57, 123, 148, 190, 193

authority 8, 16, 28, 34, 35, 47, 52, 54, 58, 63, 67, 68, 69, 72, 80, 87, 94, 126, 127, 132, 134, 135, 137, 138, 147, 148, 149, 163, 164, 165, 187, 189

## B

becoming 47, 52, 56, 69, 79, 90, 91, 98, 101, 102, 112, 129, 144, 168, 177, 181, 183

behaviorism 8, 26, 31, 34, 42, 44, 45, 47, 49, 63, 75, 77, 88, 92, 99, 107, 121, 149, 173

behaviorist 11, 12, 13, 14, 17, 26, 28, 29, 31, 32, 34, 43, 44, 45, 46, 75, 76, 78, 80, 88, 97, 99, 115, 122, 123, 174, 185

## C

capability 33, 41, 43, 46, 58, 70, 85, 92, 108, 109, 112, 115, 117, 122, 123, 138, 139, 147, 148, 149, 159, 174, 175, 176, 177, 180, 185

capacity 4, 14, 15, 19, 22, 33, 35, 40, 43, 47, 49, 64, 76, 87, 92, 99, 101, 102, 105, 107, 109, 113, 114, 115, 117, 122, 123, 124, 125, 126, 135, 138, 144, 147, 148, 150, 158, 159, 164, 165, 167, 173, 176, 179, 181, 182, 186, 188, 189, 191, 194

Colgate South Africa x, 39, 40, 42, 45, 54, 80, 84, 93, 111, 112, 113, 114, 115, 116, 121, 122, 126, 133, 134, 135, 136, 137, 138, 145, 146, 147, 148, 149, 151, 152, 160, 161, 163, 164, 166, 167, 174, 176, 177, 178, 180, 181

community 7, 9, 27, 41, 44, 46, 79, 80, 83, 93, 94, 117, 119, 122, 123, 126, 152, 162, 163, 164, 165, 175, 176, 181, 186, 188, 189, 192

conditioning 4, 16, 27, 30, 31, 33, 34, 37, 43, 45, 47, 51, 61, 63, 64, 73, 75, 76, 79, 90, 92, 93, 98, 115, 124, 132, 151, 174, 188, 191, 192, 195

consciousness 14, 16, 23, 27, 30, 46, 59, 63, 64, 71, 82, 88, 95, 108, 109, 110, 117, 122, 125, 130, 135, 144, 145, 147, 151, 152, 153, 157, 158, 159, 168, 169, 173, 178, 190

Made in the USA
Las Vegas, NV
17 October 2023

79233523R00129